# MEETING TEACHERS' MANAGEMENT NEEDS

EDUCATION AND HUMAN COMMUNICATION SERIES

PUBLISH OR PERISH: a guide for academic
authors.
Edited by Philip Hills

SUCCESSFUL WRITING.
Nancy Harrison

INFORMATION TECHNOLOGY IN THE DELIVERY
OF DISTANCE EDUCATION AND TRAINING.
Ray Winders

PUBLISHING BY MICROCOMPUTER: Problems
and Possibilities.
Tom Carney

MEETING TEACHERS' MANAGEMENT NEEDS.
Alan Bullock

# MEETING TEACHERS' MANAGEMENT NEEDS

Alan Bullock

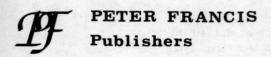

PETER FRANCIS
Publishers

© 1988 Alan Bullock

Peter Francis Publishers, Orchard House,
Berrycroft, Soham. Ely. Cambs.. CB7 5BL

British Library Cataloguing in Publication Data

Bullock, Alan
  Meeting teacher's management needs
  1. Teachers. In-service training.
  Curriculum subjects. Management
  658'.007'11

  ISBN 1-870167-05-8

Printed and bound in Great Britain by
Biddles Ltd, Guildford and Kings Lynn

# CONTENTS

Dedicated to my wife Helen,and
my daughters Margaret and Joy

# INTRODUCTION

My professional experience as head of department, a section head, deputy head and head teacher, emphasized to me the critical role of middle managers in effective school organization. Yet, many heads of department seemed frustrated in the role, lacked management skills and were confused about their role.

This book describes aspects of research carried out to discover insights into what middle managers in schools actually do, how they account for their actions and how they interact with their colleagues. At the outset of this work two assumptions were tested:

* Master Teachers, experienced and effective classroom managers, make good middle managers

* Heads of department have been trained for their roles as middle managers

Turning to the literature on the role of heads of department, it was found to be sparse. There were only two books which were of an exhortative nature. (Marland, 1971 and Marland & Hill, 1981). A series of D.E.S. publications (1977; 1979; 1981b; 1983a; 1984b; 1985b) suggested two major factors about heads of department. First, that the effectiveness of their role influenced the quality of education in schools. Second, that the majority of heads of department were in need of In-

# Introduction

Service Education. These views reinforced the feeling that heads of department were appointed with little thought on the part of L.E.A.'s, schools governors and some head teachers, as to the significance of their managerial roles, their need for training and an understanding of the difficulties which they might experience.

In order to achieve the research objective, I decided that an in-depth study of a single school over a period of time would be an effective approach. Realizing that I would become immersed in the work of heads of department with a view to understanding their difficulties, perceptions and interpretation of their expressive roles, and that a single research method with good controls would not serve this propsed research programme, I concluded that the developmental mode of enquiry practised by Glazer and Strauss provided the best means of achieving the aims of the study.

> To be sure, one goes out and studies an area with a particular sociological perspective and with a focus, a general question or a problem in mind. But (the researcher) can (and we believe should) also study an area without any preconceived theory that dictates, prior to the research, 'relevances' in concepts and hypotheses. (Glazer & Strauss, 1967)

Hudson also emphasized the importance of culling the reality of a working environment.

> My assumption is that human thought, before it is squeezed into its Sunday best for the purpose of publication is a nebulous and intuitive affair. In place of logic, there brews a stew of hunch and partial insight, well submerged. And although we accept that our minds' products must eventually be judged by the puritan rules of evidence and insight - the straight gate through which they must pass - we seem in practice to draw what insight we possess, from hidden stockpiles of images, metaphors and echoes,

2

# Introduction

ancient in origin but still growing. (Hudson, 1972)

Indeed, the role of the researcher would be akin to an anthropologist seeking to understand social reality as different people see it and to demonstrate how their views shape the action which they take within that reality. This study is known as an ethnography and the researcher, an ethnographer (see Woods, 1986)

It is hoped that in reading this work teacher practitioners will identify themselves with and show empathy towards the persons recorded in the text. A conscious decision was made to show bias in the research towards the problems of practitioners, for it was thought to be too easy to cite good practice in the hope that others will emulate similar standards of practice. Rather, let trainers and practitioners alike acknowledge the reality that master teachers may well not become effective middle managers through experience in post and it can be an effective means of learning from others' difficulties. Indeed, The importance of failure as part of the process of learning would seem to be frequently overlooked with over-emphasis on the ability to succeed, thus creating unnecessary anxiety among teachers about the possibility of failure in management practices.

A further hope is that the Government and, in turn L.E.A.'s, will acknowledge that adequate training is essential for departmental heads to deliver management of quality. Appropriate additional resources are required to enable professionally trained teachers of students to cease being amateurish managers through no fault of their own. Finally, perhaps this script may encourage other teachers to embark on an ethnographic study which will increase understanding of the management of schools and thereby contribute to the quality of education offered to current and future students in our schools.

# 1 THE HEAD OF DEPARTMENT IN SECONDARY SCHOOLS

## An Historical Approach

An historical perspective of the headteacher role inevitably spans the time since schools were established in this country, and the role of the headteacher has been well documented in literature. In contrast, the historical perspective of the head of department is found in only a limited number of publications, and, as a nationally recognized role, the head of department's role spans barely three decades.

Prior to heads of department gaining financial reward for their role in the school organization, assistant teachers had accepted from their headteachers posts of responsibility but were heads of department in name only (Gosden, 1972). The term 'head of department' was merely an informal status-tag applied within a school in an attempt to create an organizational framework for subjects within the school curriculum. Until 1945 no payment was made for the post of head of department, and until that time a head of department was an informal recognition of seniority or qualifications. In most cases, seniority at a particular school was the sole criterion for 'appointing' a head of department.

The Burnham Committee of 1945 established at national level posts of special responsibility (P.S.R.) or graded allowances, which gave headteachers the opportunity to establish

4

# The Head of Department

formal responsibilities for curriculum matters in their schools. However, although the role of head of department became officially recognized at this time, there was no immediate change in teachers' perception of the role. The graded allowances for heads of department ranged from £50 to £100 for men, and for women between £40 and £80. Sir William Alexander, writing about the Committee's Report stated that the allowances were to be granted for:

> special responsibility, work of an advanced character, professional or industrial qualifications or other circumstances, which in the opinion of the Local Authority justify an additional payment to the basic scale. (Alexander, 1954)

No mention was made of a middle management role, but in contrast there was indicated a vague notion of a master teacher who was either well qualified, who had a breadth of experience, or who could offer a shortage subject such as science.

Gosden tells us that there were few P.S.R. paid between 1945 and 1948, but in 1948 the Burnham Committee:

> laid down that these responsibility allowances should be attached to between 12.5% and 17.5% of full-time posts under each Local Authority, and that individual payments might range from £50 to £150. (Gosden, 1972)

In practice much of the responsibility for making the allocation of P.S.R. within schools was left to the discretion of headteachers, and they generally recognized advanced level teaching as the most valid reason for granting these posts. The position of head of department therefore, at this early stage in the evolution of the role, did not acquire any extra authority or managerial responsibilities from those prior to 1945.

Lacey sums up the situation at the beginning of the 1950s in

5

## The Head of Department

this way:

> The Allowance System with its graded posts and
> responsibility allowance was more a formal recognition
> of seniority and qualifications or status-confirming,
> than an authority structure. (Lacey, 1970)

Marland is more scathing with his comment that:

> There were a few chores involved; curriculum innov-
> ation was an unnecessary term and teachers were
> friends (or perhaps enemies) rather than 'colleagues'.
> An experienced teacher with a good qualification in
> his subject could be dubbed 'Senior Mathematics
> Master', the examination arrangements could be fixed
> up over coffee, and the new chap would probably learn
> from the atmosphere and a few friendly bits of
> off-the-cuff advice. (Marland, 1971)

Hilsum and Start (1974) gave a pragmatic view, suggesting
that headteachers awarded P.S.R. as an incentive to attract
or to retain valued members of staff.

The largest teachers' union, the National Union of Teachers,
whose principal aims were mirrored in the Burnham Report of
1945, continued with its cause to serve its members, the vast
majority of whom were non-graduates. It obtained a significant concession in the 1955 Burnham Report when a decision
was made about head of department posts that

> allowances should not be confined to grammar schools
> or to science teachers alone. (Tropp, 1957)

The following year, 1956, the Burnham Committee recommended a
head of department and graded allowance scheme based on the
number and ages of pupils in every school. This statistical
device is known as the 'Unit Total System', and although 1956
may be considered to be the birth of the mandatory allocation
of P.S.R. allowances, the head of department structure of

6

# The Head of Department

schools was still discretionary. Furthermore, at this time:

> It was expected that there would be a higher frequency
> of head of department posts in grammar schools
> undertaking advanced level work than in secondary
> modern schools where no advanced level work was taken.
> (Alexander, 1956)

The concept of the role of head of department in secondary schools was still embryonic with an emphasis on the head of department as a master teacher.

Some further guidelines were given in the 1956 Burnham Committee Report on the criteria to be applied in the allocation of P.S.R. having regard to

> the size of the department and its importance in the
> curriculum; to the number of teachers employed in the
> schools and to the amount of advanced level work
> undertaken. (Burnham Report, 1956, Appendix VII).

These guidelines again lacked precision in acknowledging the concept of a head of department, and Hilsum and Start sum up the situation after the 1956 salary settlement by saying that

> The important principle is that a post of head of
> department is intended to cover recognizable
> responsibilities for a subject or group of subjects
> throughout the school. (Alexander, 1957)

Those recognisable responsibilities were not specified, and headteachers were given freedom to allocate P.S.R. as they desired. Inevitably, most head of department posts were filled from within schools, and their role depended upon the incumbent's ability. In other words, a highly personalized concept of the role of the head of department prevailed at this time, and continued for some time to come. Three years later, Alexander estimated that between 50 and 75 per cent of

## The Head of Department

assistant teachers in secondary schools were in receipt of a
P.S.R., many of whom were designated head of department. In
his view, there was little thought given to a management
structure in schools when allocating P.S.R. In summary, the
salary awards recommended by Burnham Committees were accepted
by Local Authorities without careful consideration of their
effective use in schools. Financial rewards were accepted by
heads of department without defined roles and an understanding of management responsibilities.

The 1961 Burnham Report introduced an additional graded
allowance, Grade 'E', which reinforced the importance of the
head of department's role. The establishment of head of department posts and their related salary scales caused the
creation of formal hierarchies in schools, and a career
structure for teachers. However, the middle management role
of departmental heads remained in embryonic form. In his
study of comprehensive schools Monks commented that

> Often there was no clear delegation of responsibility
> for various activities, or responsibility was shared
> between several members of staff'. (Monks, 1970)

The structure of teachers' salary scales was reshaped again
in 1972 with the introduction of a 'Senior Teacher' grade.
The stress on allocating graded allowances for academic work
and organization of subject departments continued, despite
the trend towards comprehensive education and the creation
and recognition of pastoral care systems. However, it was
apparent that the head of department as master teacher remained the predominant role as opposed to a head of department fulfilling the role of a middle manager.

With a decentralized educational system operating in this
country, it was not surprising that there was variation
between and within Local Authorities in the interpretation of
Burnham Reports, and in decisions to allocate P.S.R. (see
Lindsey, 1970). Monks (1970) and Heycock (1970) also showed
in their surveys of comprehensive schools that the pattern of

# The Head of Department

distribution of heads of department posts reflected the individual school's priorities. The recipients of the highest departmental allowances were judged to be the three academic subjects, English, Mathematics and Science, but there was no other common pattern in the distribution of allowances amongst other traditional subject departments. Responsibilities written by headteachers for their heads of department ranged from vague statements such as:

> Giving the lead in matters of staff discipline and professional bearing. (Goodwin, 1963)

to a 'shopping list':

> Design a syllabus, choose text books, care for audio visual aids... (Heycock, 1970)

Lambert also concluded that:

> Any definition of role seems to have developed from the field of established practice rather than from any conscious effort to think out role definitions in relation to objectives. (Lambert, 1972)

In the 1975 Houghton Report, the current five graded allowances 'A' to 'E' were reduced to Grades I to IV, and an additional senior teacher grade was made available dependent upon the size of the Unit Total of schools. Houghton commented on the role of head of department, and thought that fundamentally the role was as vague as it had been in 1956. Graded allowances were given to teachers responsible for student pastoral care, libraries, resources and the co-ordination of extra curricular activities as well as the organization of academic subjects in the school curriculum. It was true that head of department posts were clearly 'labelled' in advertisements - 'Head of Mathematics - Scale IV', but the role 'behind' the label was often unclear. The work of Siddle (1977), focussed particularly on the role of heads of science and also came to the conclusion that there

# The Head of Department

was still much confusion on the part of headteachers as to what they required from middle management posts.

The national Secondary School Survey (D.E.S., 1979) carried out by Her Majesty's Inspectors gave a view that a great deal of in-service training was needed in this middle management role as they judged that many heads of department were not fulfilling their responsibilities. At the beginning of the 1980s the role of head of department was in one way at a critical stage in its evolution. Incumbents who had been given salary awards when they first became available will by now have left or will be about to retire from the teaching profession. A new era is about to dawn, but the question remains; are the new generation of heads of department effectively establishing the role of middle manager?

The nature of schools has radically changed both in size and in complexity over the past two decades. Curriculum development and innovation have occurred at a rapid rate. Spurred on by the work of the Schools Council during the 1960s and '70s much examination reform has taken place, culminating in the innovation of the General Certificate of Secondary Education in 1986. Over the same period of time comprehensive education has developed throughout this country. Such changes have affected the work of teachers and has inevitably affected the role of heads of department.

In the past two decades then, headteachers and their senior management teams have relied on heads of department as specialist subject teachers to interpret and innovate change both in the curriculum and in examination reform. At national level, the D.E.S. and H.M.I. assume that heads of department are middle managers as well as master teachers, but criticize them for not being equal to their role. (D.E.S., 1978; D.E.S., 1979; D.E.S., 1982; T.E.S., 1986). Many assumptions still appeared to be made about this role by a range of persons working within, and in conjunction with, the teaching profession, resulting in a vague and idiosyncratic interpretation. Furthermore as a result of prolonged teacher pay

## The Head of Department

negotiations (1985-87) the role of heads of department could have become a contractual obligation, but instead, a series of incentive allowances are available for award at the discretion of headteachers and governing bodies. The management role of heads of department remains vague, and the onus is on individual schools to define this role and interpret its significance.

## A Review of Literature and Research

In 1982, when I began research on the role of head of department in secondary schools, there were only two books specifically written on this subject, and this was still the situation last year. Research papers focussing on the role of head of department were also sparce, but during the past five years there have been a number of dissertations written on this subject. It is also significant that in January 1986, the National Foundation for Educational Research embarked upon a two year project entitled 'Middle Managemnent in Schools: Heads of Department', acknowledging that although litle attention has been given to the role of head of department, it is at the departmental level that school policy is implemented.

Ten years after publishing his first book 'The Head of Department', Marland in partnership with Hill edited a second text incorporating the views of a number of educationalists on this middle management role. A significant sentence on the first page of this second book is:

> It is clear that insufficient attention has been paid by researchers and students of educational administration, by providers of in-service training, and by those responsible for career development in schools, to the needs of heads of department. (Marland and Hill, 1981)

Hughes' research survey "Professional Development Provision

# The Head of Department

for Senior Staff in Schools and Colleges", commissioned by the D.E.S. later in the same year, confirmed the view of Marland and Hill that insufficient attention had been given to this pivotal role in schools.

The limited number of research studies on the role of head of department is annotated in an N.F.E.R. publication (Fletcher-Campbell, 1986), but a significant observation by Ribbins (1985) was that the majority of published studies on middle management in schools have been taken out of context. The studies did not show the role of head of departmemt in particular institutions nor the interaction within the role set - the head of department, his superiors and subordinates. The predominant methodology used for data collection by previous researchers has been the questionnaire to enable them to collect sufficient material in a relatively short period of time. The sole use of questionnaires in the majority of cases limited the effectiveness of the work when questions were unanswered by respondents. For example, twenty per cent of heads of department in Howson's work (1980) failed to answer the question: 'What is involved in the job of head of department?' The replies of a further twenty seven per cent did not show a discernable style of operation for their departments which left the researcher speculating an answer. Archer freely admits that although his work was potentially a worthwhile study it was

> ... limited to descriptive work that did not refer to
> any particular real situation (Archer, 1981)

Lambert (1972) seems to have been the first person in Britain to produce research evidence specifically on the role of the head of department in secondary schools. From his profession-al experience he had observed an apparent role conflict be-tween headteachers and their heads of department. To in-vestigate this concern he produced a questionnaire based upon a special report on this subject presented by his chief education officer to the Southampton Education Committee. He sought to analyse factors of role set, role expectations,

12

# The Head of Department

role perception and role conflict in order to draw some
conclusions about the actual role of head of department in a
secondary school, its definition and development, as well as
possible reasons for conflict. Lambert adapted Taylor's model
of the role for College Principals (1964).

Rational and Task Centred

INSTRUMENTAL

|  |  |
|---|---|
| (stock control, examination preparing) | (departmental policy syllabus preparation) |

INSTITUTIONAL ———————————————————— ACADEMIC

|  |  |
|---|---|
| (parental evenings, attendance at courses) | (leadership roles, departmental moderation) |

EXPRESSIVE

Affective and Person Centred

The role was sub-divided into four task areas, as shown in
the model above, and Lambert selected fifty eight tasks.
Lambert's findings showed that:

1. Where statements in the questionnaire were specific, as
   opposed to that of a general nature, there was a great
   deal of disagreement amongst, and between, headteachers
   and their heads of department concerning the role of a
   head of department. This reflected not only the role
   ambiguity of the head of department's role, but also the
   individual nature of English schools in a devolved system
   of education.

2. The instrumental academic tasks of heads of department
   were accepted by both headteachers and heads of

# The Head of Department

department, leading him to think that these should be the basis of the role of a head of department.

3. In the Expressive Academic quadrant of the model Lambert found that any task involving supervision or control of staff caused heads of department concern, but he did not give any reasons for this finding. There was considerable difference of views about these tasks within both groups surveyed and amongst heads of department, the expressive academic roles presented the greatest evidence of role conflict and role ambiguity. Lambert concluded this section of his work by saying that:

> It would seem that considerably more attention needs to be paid to expressive roles of the head of department and that the present assumption of a consensus of agreement on the role is largely mistaken. (Lambert, 1972)

4. Headteachers expected heads of department to play a greater part in controlling the staff in their department than the heads of department were prepared to accept.

Following Lambert's work other researchers reinforced aspects of his findings. The lack of role clarity and role ambiguity were emphasized by a number of writers, for example, Hall and Thomas, 1977; Siddle, 1977; England, 1980; Midgley, 1980; Bailey, 1981; Brydson, 1983; Chamberlain, 1984 and Ribbins, 1985. It was apparent from other researchers that frequently heads of department found themselves in stressful circumstances. (Dunham, 1978; Bloomer, 1980; Randle, 1984) These circumstances arose through role conflict; the supervision of colleagues who claimed professional autonomy (Hall and Thomas, 1977); the conflict of expectations between heads of department and their superiors and subordinates (England, 1980); and, in part, the lack of time given to fulfil the role of head of department. (Dunham, 1978; England, 1980; Chamberlain, 1984; and Randle, 1984)

## The Head of Department

Other significant aspects of the role of head of department
have been raised by various researchers. For example, staff
appraisal by Bailey (1981) and Straker (1984), staff
development by Brown (1984) and delegation by Chamberlain
(1984) were identified as critical issues, but these were not
contextualized within institutions. The lack of time available to heads of department for management roles was often
referred to in research papers (for example, England (1980);
Chamberlain, 1984; Randle, 1984; Straker, 1984; Waters,
(1985). However, the training provision for heads of department identified by Ribbins (1985) as an area of concern
was not pursued by other researchers. Siddle (1977) and Smith
(1977) had concluded that there was a great need for management training for those who had been promoted to middle
management roles, but no specific areas had been identified.
The training needs of heads of department remained an unanswered topic as indeed, why heads of department should
consider the evaluation of their departments to be un-
important. (Howson, 1980)

From the evidence above it is clear that much research work
still remains to be done to probe more deeply into the role
of head of department in secondary schools. The expressive,
or person centred, roles of the head of department appeared
to be the most contentious and problematic area of concern
for both head teachers and heads of department. It is in this
expressive role of managing people that heads of department
were unsure of themselves and where pevious researchers (for
example, Lambert, 1972; Siddle, 1977; Howson, 1980; Archer,
1981) found that many questions remained unanswered in their
data collection by questionnaire. It is this area that my
research focussed.

15

# 2 THE CHANGING ROLE OF HEAD OF DEPARTMENT

## A Role Concept

The terms 'role ambiguity', 'role clarity', 'role conflict' and 'role set' are used throughout. It is appropriate, therefore, that consideration, albeit brief, is given to the concept role and its related significance to the role of head of department in this study. In the literature on the concept of 'role', writers such as Newcombe (1957) and Sarbin (1968) have commented upon the inconsistencies and lack of clarity of definitions of role concept. In its simplest form, the idea of role may be explained by the analogy of an actor on the stage who acts-out the script given to him. Within the prescribed text, he will, because of his unique personality and talent, add his own individual personal interpretation and emphasis to the role. However, the role is independent of the actor; it has as it were, been prescribed for him, and in these 'prescriptions' is the basis upon which role theory is developed. Teasing out the many definitions of the concept role in order to classify them, Hughes (1972) suggested three categories; role ex- pectation of others, role as self expectation and a third category, role as actual behaviour.

Although these categories are useful in considering the comprehensive nature of the concept of role, it is important to recognize their inter-relatedness, and to note that most writers acknowledge that a holistic perspective is not

possible. In this study role is interpreted from the stand-
point of role expectation of others, self expectation and the
actual behaviour of heads of department. In their work on the
school superintendent's role, Gross et al (1966) confirmed
the usefulness of role theory, but emphasized the importance
of clearly stating the meanings of the concept in particular
cases. It was Alexander's desire

> ... that the nature of responsibility in each post
> (head of department) should be clearly stated;
> (Alexander, 1957)

but at both national and local levels role definitions of
heads of department have been vague. The work of Monks
(1970), Heycock (1970), Nash (1971) and Bailey (1981) also
confirm the lack of role clarity, thus creating role
ambiguity for heads of department. The fact that the role of
head of department is evolving has created difficulties in
stating precisely their role, but in considering the concept
of department in the next section, aspects of this role will
be highlighted such as appraiser, delegator and evaluator.

A leadership role is an inevitable perspective of a head of
department, and, more specifically, curriculum leader, will
be briefly considered. To conclude his section, the issue of
role conflict, built into the role of head of department,
will be reviewed, followed by the significance of their work
within a profession.

## Literature on Leadership

It is assumed in this study that a head of department has a
leadership role to fulfil, but, in the voluminous literature
on leadership, not all concepts, research and theories may be
relevant to school management practice. For example, the work
of Hodgkinson (1983) raises a thought-provoking philosophical
approach to leadership which elevates an awareness of the
political forces within an organization's environment. Bailey

# The Changing Role of Head of Department

(1981) and Hoyle (1982) also discuss similar issues, thereby pitching the role of leadership in a context of reality, intimating that many motives, skills and techniques are subsumed within the context of leadership.

Reflecting upon the textbook theory of organizations, it is important to recognize that formal organizational theory assumes that there are clear goals and that decisions are made on the basis of these goals. (See Burrell and Morgan, 1979). However,

> a rational view of organizations encapsulated by
> organizational theory cannot be assumed. (Hoyle, 1982)

and, therefore, it is important that the concept of leadership should always be considered in the 'real' context in which it operates. It is also important to emphasize that the concept of leadership, like that of department, is a dynamic concept and should not be thought of in a stereotyped or static way. The style of leadership will vary from person to person, and from school to school, but the techniques of leadership need to be acquired and practised in the process of managing a department.

## Curriculum Leader and Leading Professional

A common assumption found in the D.E.S. literature, (D.E.S., 1977a; 1979; 1983a; 1985), is that heads of department are curriculum leaders who will develop and maintain standards of education in schools. Within the role of curriculum leader is that of him as leading professional, involved in the responsibilities of staff development, guidance and support. Implicit in the publications of G.C.S.E. Subject Guides for Teachers (O.U. Press, 1986) is also the belief that heads of department have the role of curriculum innovator.

Three of the four main areas considered in a Government White Paper (1985b) "Better Schools", relate to the head of

18

# The Changing Role of Head of Department

department as curriculum leader. They are

1) To secure greater clarity about the objective and
     context of the curriculum.

2) To improve assessment so that it promotes more
     effectively the objectives of the curriculum and the
     achievement of pupils.

3) To improve the professional effectiveness of
     teachers and the management of the teaching force.

It may be assumed that the improvement of professional effectiveness and the management of departmental members will
involve heads of department in management practices such as
assessment, delegation, evaluation, innovation, team building
and teacher appraisal. These management skills will be referred to in the section on departmental concepts on page 23
when considering the concept 'department'. To secure greater
clarity about the objective and context of the curriculum
presupposes an understanding of the whole school curriculum
as well as the specialist knowledge of a department's contribution to the whole, and also effective leadership
qualities amongst fellow professionals.

From the work of Coulson (1984) probationary teachers desired
their head of department to have an exemplary role as leading
professional, and curriculum leadership is expected of heads
of department in supportong new enrants into the teaching
profession (D.E.S., 1982). It was also thought that 'Teachers
who need to work outside their main subject specialism will
need considerable support and guidance from the appropriate
head of department' (D.E.S., 1985b). Such are the demands,
expectations and assumptions made about the role of head of
department which point to them as middle managers, but also
master teacher who is effective in the classroom and in
managing other teachers in curriculum matters.

19

# The Changing Role of Head of Department

## Master Teacher and Middle Manager

The research studies of Lambert (1972), Siddle (1977), Howson (1980) and Archer (1981) confirm that role ambiguity of the head of department's role is much in evidence, thus causing role conflict. Headteachers and L.E.A. Officers' expectations were in conflict with those of heads of department, and heads of department did not agree amongst themselves about their role.

Another dimension of potential role conflict has been highlighted by Hughes in Bush et al (1980) and in an earlier work (Hughes, 1975), when he suggested the reconciling of professional and administrative roles of professional educators. He argued, as did Etzioni (1964), that such a dual role can be a very effective way of lessening conflict in professionally staffed organizations. Therefore, although role conflict may be concentrated in an individual, 'the greater good' may be experienced by the organization. In contrast, Handy (1984), who claimed to know something of organization theory but little of schools, completed a survey of schools for a Schools Council Project. He formed the opinion that it would be wise to have leading professionals and administrators, but unwise to combine the two roles in one person because it would be an invitation to stress.

The additional built-in role conflict for heads of department of master teacher and middle manager must be added to the dimensions already described above. A major reason for this particular role conflict would appear to be the limited amount of time allocated to heads of department to fulfil the dual roles of master teacher and middle manager.

> Heads of department in all the schools (Norfolk
> secondary schools) had insufficient time for
> monitoring the work of their departments, supervising
> the work of other teachers and planning and bringing
> about new developments. (D.E.S., 1984b)

# The Changing Role of Head of Department

In his survey of schools, Handy concludes that

> secondary schools seem to have inherited the
> managerial traditions ... appropriate to smaller and
> simpler places. They are trying to run large and
> complex role cultures in their spare time. It can't be
> done - not with any hope of success. (Handy, 1984)

The management of time may be an essential skill for a middle
manager to acquire, but it would appear that heads of department are given the task of fulfilling 'the art of the
impossible' (Marland, 1971). Acknowledging that, on average,
an eighty per cent teaching commitment as master teacher was
unreasonable if a middle management role also is to be fulfilled, a question must be posed: are heads of department
prepared and trained as middle managers? Lack of training and
inept practice in management techniques will add to the
intensity of stress to the built-in role conflicts for heads
of department evolved over the past three decades.

## Professionalism

Consideration is now given to the fact that teachers are
members of a profession. Hughes says of the concept of
professionalism:

> Profession, like leadership, is an elusive concept and
> is a word with variation of meaning in the social
> science literature, and even more so in general usage.
> (Hughes, 1985)

Millerson (1984) catalogued twenty three distinct traits
which have been recorded in definitions of the concept
profession; but the purpose here is to highlight those traits
of professionalism which may have bearing on understanding
the significance of the role of head of department. A stance
of privacy is a hallmark of the traditions of professionalism (Hoyle, 1975), and such a trait runs counter to

21

# The Changing Role of Head of Department

an effective open role culture within an organization. In writing about the teaching profession, Handy says:

> Certainly the traditions of professionalism remain strong. Tenure, the privacy of the classroom and the right to express one's own views in one's own ways, the sense of accountability primarily to one's own profession - these are all hallmarks of a profession and of a person culture ... They (the hallmarks of a profession) do not sit well with graded hierarchies, standardized curricula and the management ethos of a large institution, all of which call for a role culture. (Handy, 1984)

Clearly, professional autonomy would have an effect on the role of head of department as staff developer and appraiser. It is significant, however, that Shipman (1983) asserts that in order to maintain professional autonomy he believes that the teaching profession should effectively exercise the practice of evaluation.

Hall (1968) found that a professional desire for autonomy resulted in a negative reaction towards bureaucracy, division of labour and hierarchical authority. In other words, teachers as professionals are likely to claim professional freedom in a range of activites which may also include their own in-service education. Hoyle (1974) makes a useful distinction between professionalism and professionality, suggesting that the latter is linked with improving professional practice, and that professionalism is associated with status. He then goes on to argue that some teachers are 'restricted professionals' whilst others respond to an 'extended professionality': namely, they are involved in in-service work and value professional collaboration. (See Hoyle in Bush et al, 1980.) The extent to which teachers are prepared to be collaborative and available to receive training will affect all members of the head of department role set, and, consequently, their perception of the role of head of department.

## The Changing Role of Head of Department

Gordon et al (1985) open up a debate "Is Teaching a Profession?", which is taken up by Hoyle who tentatively concludes that

> this voice (the teaching profession) would probably be strengthened if the education profession, rather than the teaching profession was able to develop a set of more widely shared values. But such a situation could probably only arise if there was a reconsideration of patterns of training, career structure, salary structure and criteria for promotions. (Hoyle, 1969a)

Based on the evidence provided in this chapter, career structure, patterns of training, salary structure and criteria for promotion would certainly seem to have much bearing on the present concept of the role of head of department.

## A Departmental Concept

As no clear role definition of head of department could be found in research papers or in the review of literature on this subject, it was important to sharpen up this concept in readiness for proceeding with a research ethnographic study. I thought that an understanding of the concept 'department' would give a focussed insight of the role of head of department. Within a secondary school, a department may be simply equated with the term 'subject', referring to the provision of one part of the school's curriculum such as Biology, History or Religious Education. Such an interpretation is simplistic and shallow, and a comprehensive perspective is required considering a number of facets beginning with the concept, organization.

## Organization

A department is sometimes explained as a sub-unit of the school's organization and this interpretation of a department

# The Changing Role of Head of Department

will depend upon an understanding of an organization.

> Perspectives derive from cultures. They do not exist,
> nor are they created in a vacuum. (Woods, 1983,)

Most schools have a hierarchical structure, 'a time-honoured
form of organization for getting work done' (Packwood, 1977),
with heads of department working in the middle eschelon of
the hierarchy. Heads of departments' perceptions of how
organizations operate may well determine their modus operandi
and their concept of a department. A structuralist systems
perspective of an organization deems people as existing
independently of the organization. However, Silverman (1970)
and Greenfield (1975 and 1980) challenged the systems theor-
ist approach because of its failure to take into account the
perceptions of individual members of an organization. They
emphasized the importance of individuals working within an
organization and favoured an interactionalist perpective
where individuals are involved in negotiation about their
work in the organization.

The consequences of practising the theory of differing
paradigms of organizations will result in varying concepts of
a department, its mode of operation, the role of departmental
members and the perspective of a department as a sub-unit of
an organization. The structuralist systems approach is likely
to produce a mechanistic management system with a fixed hierarchical structure as opposed to the interactionalist
approach which is likely to engender consultation and understanding amongst members and an organic form of management
system (See Burns and Stalker, 1968). Such modes of
management will colour the concept of department and the role
of head of department.

Following the Hawthorne studies (Encyclopaedia of Educational
Research, 1982), industrial psychologists came to recognize
that within formal organizations, informal structures were
created, and that these structures influence the manner in
which members of departments fulfil their roles. It was found

## The Changing Role of Head of Department

that structures can play a major part in meeting the emotional needs of members, their motivation to work and the quality of work achieved. A department, therefore, should not be viewed just as a formal organizational unit, for within departments informal structures can develop according to group dynamics. Organizational theorists (see MacGregor, 1960; Katz and Kahn, 1966; Paisey, 1980; Schmuck and Runkel, 1986) developed complex models which attempt to include relationships between departments and their environments. These models do not have the simplicity and neatness of the classical organizational model, but they are possibly nearer to reality, for departments do interact with their environment in complex ways.

## People

'Organization is people not things' (Paisey, 1981), and it is important to recognize that the beliefs and uncertainties of people about organization reflect their relationships with others in an organization. These human relationships will colour the concept of department, and Hoyle describes the underlying motives and attitudes of participants within an organization as 'an organizational underworld, the world of micropolitics'. (Hoyle, 1986) The importance of micropolitics has been discussed by other writers, (see Maughan, 1979; Bailey, 1982; Glatter, 1982), and highlights that a department is a dynamic concept and not a static one.

It is interesting to note that many text books on management and organizations assume that people are rational and act accordingly to rational principles. The study of micropolitics emphasizes that people act with prejudice and bias to further their own interests, (see Hoyle, 1982) and do not always act in a rational manner. This image of people, 'warts and all', leads one to realism of departmental membership. Furthermore, from a pragmatic viewpoint, in answer to the question, 'what is a department?', Richardson says:

25

# The Changing Role of Head of Department

> It is not even a group of teachers, for this would
> imply that every member of staff belonged to one
> department. The possibilitiues of splitting, and
> projection within a 'system' of departments are
> enormous. (Richardson, 1973)

Indeed, within the day-to-day reality of a school a head of
department can never expect to manage a group of teachers
solely committed to the work of one department, and each of
them will bring their strengths and weaknesses to the
department's work.

## Delegation

From another perspective, McGivering argued that:

> A department does not automatically come into
> existence just because more than one person teaches a
> given subject; it exists only when deliberate
> collaboration begins. (McGivering, 1971)

It is assumed that an integral part of the act of collaboration is an agreed division of labour amongst departmental
members, and this will come about through the practice of
delegation. In other words, departmental objectives can best
be achieved if departmental members accept responsibility for
tasks within a co-ordinated departmental structure.

Subsumed within this perspective of the concept of department
are assumptions that heads of department will practise
various management skills and involve departmental members.
The skills of negotiation are an integral part of the
practice of delegation (Steinmetz, 1985; Handy, 1984), and
the problems and experience of negotiators apply equally to
delegators. For example, a reduction in heads of departments'
control will occur in the course of delegation, but a framework may be created in which both departmental members and
whole departments may develop. However, it is important not

26

# The Changing Role of Head of Department

whole departments may develop. However, it is important not to give the impression that effective negotiation nor delegation will necessarily bring tranquility with goodwill overflowing from departmental members. There will always be a tension between meeting individual needs and departmental demands; a potential source of conflict for every delegator.

On delegation Watts feels that 'The crucial question is that of where the decisions are made and to whom decision-makers are accountable.' (Watts, in Bush et al., 1980) This question raises many issues related to the dynamic concept of department - the day-to-day work of a department. These issues can range from the status of heads of department and their trust in departmental members, to the requirement of accountability. Furthermore, the management skills of delegation like that of negotiation can create the climate in which evaluation and appraisal, innovation and team work may develop. Certainly the effective process of negotiation and delegation will bring heads of department into a close working relationship with colleagues and highlight yet other factors which create the concept of department, such as appraisal and evaluation.

# Appraisal and Evaluation

Within the concept of department are many integral management activities which give life and reality to the secondary school department. The monitoring and controlling process of a department may be organized by a person or group of people with authority. This authority can eminate from an autocratic style of management of a departmental head at one end of the spectrum, or from the self discipline of dedicated pro-fessional departmental members at the other.

In most school organizations authority is embodied in an hierarchical post, which for the school department is the head of department. In a school's hierarchy every head of department may expect a defined area of responsibility and

## The Changing Role of Head of Department

should have the authority to implement delegated tasks from a higher authority - the head teacher - to ensure that the standards of departmental activities are maintained. Within this context the practices of appraisal and evaluation may operate to gain feedback on the quality of the department's work.

There is a growing body of literature on the subject of staff appraisal, for example, Beveridge, 1975; Bailey, 1981; Philip, 1983; King, 1984; N.A.H.T., 1985; Suffolk Education Department, 1985 and 1987. In addition, the "Illuminative" (Parlett and Hamilton, 1972) or "Responsive" model of evaluation (Stake, 1980) acknowledges the complexity of educational settings and the unintended consequences of curriculum programmes (see Simon, 1980). Indeed, formative evaluation can heighten the awareness of the process of educational activities, create an awareness of the dynamic nature of a department and the significance of the role of head of department as appraiser and evaluator.

## Change and Innovation

Implied in a dynamic perspective of a department is its growth: the department ideally generating its own creative thinking and innovation. Effective planned change requires a great deal of expertise from a head of department, with co-operation, adaptability and understanding from department-al members, as together they develop the capacity to meet a variety of new problems. Curriculum development which inevitably causes change and innovation has been described as 'a professional activity, consciously and deliberately carried by teachers and others' (D.E.S., 1985a), but not all departments may have the capacity to manage successfully change and innovation, especially if heads of department lack the managerial skills necessary to manage change.

An alternative set of circumstances is haphazard change, described as 'organizational drift': 'That is, organizations evolve, adjust and re-adjust, seemingly unaffected by the conscious efforts of the members'. (Wheeler, 1973)

Since a department is ever changing in nature, a head of department will require an understanding of change and the expertise to monitor the effects of innovation. There is a plethora of literature on this complex subject, for example (Chin and Benne, 1969; Havelock, 1969; Hoyle, 1970; Gross, 1971; Harris, 1976; Gray, 1982; Fullan, 1985) which highlight the importance of preparation for innovation, dissemination of data and the period of 'after care' following the innovation. For change to be effective all persons involved must find meaning in both the content and the process of that change.

The consequence of poor management of innovation, can well result in 'tissue rejection', (Hoyle, 1970) when the proposed innovation fails to become a reality. Indeed, the idea of 'planting' an idea, concept or innovation from outside a departmental organization, sharply focusses the concept of a department as a seedbed where there is potential growth. The effectiveness of a department reflects the capability of the human response to specific innovations and change; co-operation and adaptability of departmental members and heads of department with the skills to manage effectively. The role of innovator and manager of change would appear to be an integral part of a role definition of head of department.

## Team Work

Team work encapsulates the concept of department, and writing in "Ten Good Schools" H.M.I. made the following comment about team work:

   It is a feature of all these schools that much
   attention has been given to departmental or faculty
   organization and that the staff spend a considerable
   amount of time in planning and discussing their

> courses ... The general level of competence of shared
> understanding and purpose made for an evenness of
> achievement and is commendable (D.E.S., 1977a)

This quotation may appear bland, but it is significant; to
create a balanced and coherent team of professional teachers
is a more subtle business than is commonly realized.

Trust between team members is the bedrock upon which
interpersonal skills may develop, and a means of creating a
cohesive team where people are recognized as having different
personalities, attitudes, strengths and weaknesses. Paisey's
statement about organizations is also relevant to departmental teams: 'Organization exists when two or more
people share a common purpose. It persists as long as the
common purpose is retained.' (Paisey, 1981) It is not
surprising, therefore, that Hargreaves thought that

> The head of department's first task is to weld into a
> team the diverse members of the department so that
> they can collaborate in sharing ideas, experience,
> knowledge and skills for the benefit of their teaching
> and the pupil's learning. (I.L.E.A., 1984)

The environment in which 'effective teams recognize both
personal and group needs' (Handy, in Bush et al., 1980) will
not occur by chance, but need to be created by heads of
department in dialogue with their departmental team. A
department being a human oeganization, cognisance has to be
given to

> The strategies by which individuals and groups in
> organizational contexts seek to use their resources of
> power and influence to their own interests. (Hoyle,
> 1982)

A department, then, is a 'living' unit within an organization
and is a dynamic concept. A department has a prime function,

# The Changing Role of Head of Department

and in a school, this is to provide education for students. A department may comprise any number of persons greater than one, and when the efforts of these persons are co-ordinated, they can be more effective than one of them alone in achieving the functions of the department. A simplistic static view of a department does not reflect the complexities of interaction between departmental members and their environment in a changing world. These factors have an effect on and affect the role of a head of department for which post holders require training in order to acquire management skills.

## Management Training

It is reasonable to suggest that effective management training may only be planned if the role definition of heads of department is clear. Previous sections of this chapter have shown that the role of head of department is evolving and manifests role ambiguity and role conflict. One can therefore only speculate upon what training is appropriate for heads of department and what are the key areas of this training.

From a randon sample of schools, L.E.A.'s and institutions of Higher Education courses, a lack of provision for preparing potential and in-post heads of department for the role of head of department was noted. This situation may not be surprising as the role definition is unclear, but it is also significant to highlight the mismatch between the D.E.S. and H.M.I. expectations of heads of department and the provision made at national level for effective management training. Unfortunately, it has been assumed by H.M.I. and the D.E.S. for at least the past two decades that sooner rather than later the major training needs of heads of department will be given a high profile and provision made to improve the performance of the majority of them. During the last decade there has been an intense communication of expectations, either explicit or implicit, in the form of criticism of poor management or exhortations of what should be good practice.

# The Changing Role of Head of Department

Examples of these statements are legion. In a national Secondary School Survey 'H.M.I. identified In-Service training for heads of department as a priority in one-third of the schools visited ...'(D.E.S., 1979) In the Cockcroft Report it is stated:

> If the current standards of mathematical education are
> to be improved, the raising of the quality of
> leadership at this level (departmental) may be the
> most important single factor. (Cockcroft, 1982)

In the Government White Paper, "Teaching Quality"

> Only if they (staff with management responsibilities
> within schools) are effective managers of their
> teaching staffs ... possessing the qualities needed
> for effective educational leadership, can schools
> offer their pupils the quality of education which they
> have the right to expect. (D.E.S., 1983a)

A final example in another White Paper, entitled "Better Schools", under a sub-heading, "The Need for Action", it is recorded that:

> The Government has a duty to act where it can ... to
> improve the professional effectiveness of teachers and
> the management of the teaching force. (D.E.S., 1985a)

Most of these statements made in these publications about middle management practice are of a general nature and include planning, consultation and evaluation of staff, which it was believed would contribute greatly to the enhancement of effective management. (See D.E.S., 1977a; D.E.S., 1979; D.E.S., 1983a, and Welsh Office, 1984). The production of a scheme of work was considered to be most important. Contingent upon the implementation of schemes of work was the guidance of departmental staff and the assessment of work achieved. The induction of probationary teachers into the teaching profession (D.E.S., 1982) was also thought to be an

32

# The Changing Role of Head of Department

important role of heads of department. An extension of this
management practice, the appraisal of other departmental
colleagues was highlighted in "Teaching Quality" (D.E.S.,
1983a) and again two years later in a booklet, "Quality in
Schools: Evaluation and Appraisal" (D.E.S., 1985b). The
importance of this particular management practice is also
given prominence in Part IV of the 1986 Education Act.

Such are samples of the areas of management the D.E.S. and
H.M.I. are desiring from middle managers in schools. But
these expectations have not been matched by Government INSET
provision for heads of department. For example, in 1981,
Hughes was commissioned by the D.E.S. to produce a survey of
INSET provision for senior staff in schools and colleges but
his brief did not include heads of department. Senior staff
included only headteachers and their deputies, and therefore
when the Government announced in Circular 3/83 (see pp. 1 -
2) that it would fund management training as a high priority,
heads of department were not specifically included in this
provision. In his survey, Hughes found the provision of
management courses to be minimal, providing for only about
one per cent of eligible heads and their deputies. Numerical-
ly there are many more heads of department than headteachers;
how much more inadequate then would be the provision for
heads of department?

This state of affairs seems rather puzzling when the D.E.S.
acknowledged that

>    It is the head of department next to headteachers who
>    have as a group potentially the greatest influence on
>    the quality of work within a comprehensive school.
>    (Welsh Office, 1984)

From an examination of the D.E.S. Long and Short Courses
Booklets, the management provision for middle managers
remains inadequate. A ray of hope that this present situation
may change in the future is the influence of the result of a

# The Changing Role of Head of Department

current N.F.E.R. project where attention is drawn to 'The important role middle management can play in encouraging or obstructing curricular and other desired changes'. (Educ. Research News, No. 44, 1986)

The concept management 'had never been a very good or easily defined word', (Handy, 1984), as it is concerned with both objective and subjective phenomena, and as management deals with human beings, it can never be completely scientific and must, therefore, be regarded partly as an art. Indeed, management is a complex human activity whether the viewpoint is that of an individual person or that of a group of people in action as a management team, involving values, attitudes, techniques and behavioural patterns. However, management, in essence, is about getting things done. In schools there has tended to be an emphasis on individual achievement by staff and students, and, therefore, to redress this balance, management may be defined as achieving objectives with a group of people of different types of ability, each able to contribute towards an end-product.

For the purpose of my study, management training should be understood as being concerned with changing the behaviour of heads of department, and behind the phrase, 'training needs', the emphasis is on management being a practical activity; techniques, skills and principles which need to be practised. Against this background, it is important that management techniques and skills are not too exclusive or given an inflated status. The ability for curriculum planning and organization is considered to be of a high order, and it is not intended that excessive stress be placed on means as against ends of the educational process. This would devalue the professional confidence of the teacher in the classroom. Too narrow a definition of management training can also lead to an over-emphasis on the administrative and executive responsibilities of the role, and minimize a collaborative concept of management with the head of department aware of his department's contribution to the school's development vis-a-vis the contribution of other departments.

# The Changing Role of Head of Department

Under the Grant Related In-Service Education for Teachers scheme devolved to Local Authorities by the D.E.S. with effect from April 1987, the assumptions are made that:

a) Effective courses for middle managers in secondary schools will be provided.

b) Trainers have attained knowledge of the major training needs of heads of department in order to plan effective training courses for them.

It is hoped that the findings of my research will clarify the role of heads of department and highlight their training needs, thus making a contribution to effective training courses for potential heads of department as well as in-post heads of department.

# 3  EMERGING ISSUES

## A Pilot Study

The main purposes of a pilot study before embarking upon an
ethnographic study were to obtain not only insight into the
problems experienced by heads of department in the course of
their work, but also to gain confidence in administering
unstructured interviews. During the process of this work the
intention was to probe paradoxes and problems perceived by
heads of department as well as the assumptions they made when
discussing their work. This data, it was hoped, would provide
possible avenues along which research might develop. Taylor's
quadrant model described on page 13 was used to sift the data
collected into a coherent and manageable form and to test the
results of previous research.

I wrote to five headteachers of schools A - E, making a
request to interview five heads of department in each school
and to discuss their role, with a view to ascertaining what
they did in their day-to-day work. Only one question would be
asked at the outset of every interview: 'Tell me what you do
as a head of department?' All these schools had a great deal
in common, but they were different in size, catchment areas,
traditions and style of leadership. The choice of those heads
of department to be interviewed was left to the discretion of
the headteachers. At the end of every session of interviews

## Emerging Issues

the headteacher was engaged in discussion about his choice of interviewee.

The criteria devised by headteachers when selecting heads of department for interview were as follows:

a. 'They have taught for at least three years in this school.'

b. 'The heads of department are effective practitioners.'

c. 'They are experienced people...'

d. 'I was confident that they would put up a good show!'

e. 'They happened to be free from a teaching commitment on the day of the interview.'

f. 'Heads of department who were willing to take part in the research.'

One hour was allocated for every interview which included:

a) time to put the interviewee at ease; to ensure that the purpose of the interview was understood, and to give assurance of the confidentiality and anonymity

b) 40 minutes taped interview

c) a short session at the conclusion of the interview when interviewees might make additional comments on their work.

Throughout the interviews, I made the assumption that my guiding principle would be to adopt the role of 'acceptable

# Emerging Issues

incompetent' (Lofland, 1971), no assumptions having been made about the role of heads of department. Frequently interviewees paused durimg the course of interview or at the conclusion of sessions to ask 'Is this O.K.?, or 'Is this what you wanted?'. Another question which a number of interviewees asked me was 'What else do you want to know?. These are natural questions in the circumstances, and the standard answer given to the latter question was: 'Whatever else you may wish to share with me'. When interviewees declared that they had nothing further to share, on occasons just a few minutes into the interview, a summary of what had been said to date frequently triggered off the interviewee into giving further details about areas already covered, but in greater depth. By pausing and causing the interviewee to think was another method of generating a flow of data; or sometimes this was achieved by repeating the last phrase used by the interviewees. At the conclusion of taped sessions, I made notes on the after-thoughts of heads of department in my fieldwork diary. These comments were often of a strictly confidential nature, involving working relationships with colleagues. The experience of gaining this further data highlighted the potential of the ongoing nature of a study, enabling me to gather critical data when a rapport had been built up. Such an ongoing relationship was of course not possible in the pilot study.

When a set of five head-of-department interviews was completed in every school, an analysis of the taped interview was made by marking a grid to highlight recognizable patterns of role, warranting further study during either the remaining inter- views of the pilot study or the following research. This list of topics compiled from all the topics raised by interviewees was not an exhaustive catalogue. Not one of the twenty five interviewees, for example, mentioned any links with industry, work with professional bodies or links with higher education. In considering an interpretation of the analysis of this data I considered it sufficient to comment only on issues which might have potential for further investigation, bearing in mind the data from previous

38

## Emerging Issues

research findings. Comments are made now on the findings in each sector of Taylor's quadrant model.

## An Analysis of the Pilot Study Data Collection

### The instrumental/academic roles

The main issues arising in this sector were

a) Aims and objectives

In interviews the phrase 'aims and objectives' was rarely used or discussed. When it was introduced, the interviewees saw little connection between the departmental aims and objectives and those of the school, thus underlining an isolationist stance projected by many heads of department.

b) Curriculum development and innovation

Involvement in these activities was accepted as an inevitable part of the head of department's role, but seemed 'hedged around' with personal problems:

> I need to take the initiatives, try out new ideas and gradually introduce them ... getting members of the department to think my way ... of course I must be diplomatic!

The depth of understanding about the concept of innovation and the management of change was generally shallow, and therefore was registered as a topic for further consideration. Financing these activities was thought by most heads of department to be their greatest problem.

c) Management

Problems related to this subject are illustrated by such

# Emerging Issues

comments as:

> The most difficult thing is dealing with people; is
> getting them to do things which ought to be done
> without putting their backs up.

> I would like to be on the bridge and give orders, but
> it is not so easy as that because you've got to live
> with them (departmental members).

These two brief quotations speak for themselves, and occurred
in one form or another in each of the twenty five interviews.

### d) The management of time

Another topic raised many times by interviewees was the
management of time. The comments, 'I try to keep up with
curriculum innovation, but find it difficult - almost
impossible', and another comment 'I have to run in order to
stand still', suggested either an unreasonable workload
and/or a lack of skills in the management of time.

> There's a lot more work to do now than ever before
> ... I mean general admin. ... there's so much
> pressure ... something has to go, and I often find
> that my teaching is squeezed out.

This particular quotation highlighted the role conflict
experienced by heads of department, but also that the quality
of classroom practice was affected through the pressure
experienced by interviewees.

## The instrumental/institutional roles

The data in this sector suggested that this is the area where
heads of department gained their greatest job satisfaction,
namely the non-interpersonal activities such as caring for
stock, being in charge of requisitions, preparing for student

## Emerging Issues

examination entries. The issues arising were

 a) Lack of funds

Difficulties were experienced in the distribution of finances reflecting problems in prioritizing limited resources.

 b) Safety requirements

This topic was dependent upon the head of department's responsibility for equipment with potential safety hazards.

 c) Job description

Only three interviewees made mention of this subject, and the following quotation illustrates the insignificance given to the maagement role of senior colleagues by heads of department in detailing the outcome of their responsibilities 'Frankly I do not need a job description ... I think I know what the head expects ...' The attitude of heads of department towards the purpose of job description reflected an isolationist position they created for themselves.

 d) Staff development

This topic raised concern amongst heads of department, possibly due to the lack of negotiating skills they possessed when dealing with colleagues. Another salient factor was the implications of teachers practising a professional autonomy which distanced themselves from each other.


## The expressive/institutional roles

Comparing the responses of heads of department about their expressive roles with their instrumental roles, it was clear that the difficulties created by the former centred on the fact that they lacked management skills.

# Emerging Issues

Problems arising were

a) A lack of confidence

In many instances an inability to cope with expressive roles was declared by heads of department. This concern had been raised by previous researchers, for example, Siddle (1977), Howson (1980), Archer (1981); but no reasons were given for these circumstances, possibly because the method of data collection was by questionnaire. However, a frequent reason given to me for not attempting a specifc task, or finding it problematic was the lack of time available. A telling remark by one head of department who had been fired with enthusiasm whilst attending a four days' management course was: 'Alas, after four weeks of being back (at school) in reality again, there's no time to operate all the good ideas (imparted on the course).'

This suggested that either the management course lacked reality, the head of department lacked the ability to order his priorities. or not enough time was made available to the head of department. I sensed that the interviewee lacked the management skills to implement the ideas gained from his course and this created a lack of confidence to try to effect these skills. He found himself frustrated and in a catch 22 situation.

b) Attendance at professional courses

The main reason given for attendance on courses was to assist in furthering their chances of promotion; '... it always looks good on an application form ...' was one person's view. The choice of the course attended was self determined, and no mention was made of senior staff giving guidance on the professional development of colleagues. The perceived liaison which heads of department had with senior colleagues seemed only to involve routine instrumental roles.

42

## Emerging Issues

### c) A nagging doubt

A doubt developed in my mind that heads of department gave
the issue of time as an excuse to conceal areas of weakness,
lack of training skills, or confidence to deal with human
situations. It appeared that many departmental heads had
failed to cross the 'professional thresholds' to become
middle managers. They gave the impression of feeling
uncomfortable when involved with their expressive roles. This
was highlighted by the comparative silence on such topics as
staff appraisal and staff development, as well as the
problems experienced by 'limited time' and 'trusting
professionals to get on with their job'. The two latter
issues were used as reasons why expressive roles had not been
attempted or why heads of department considered that they had
failed to achieve them.

### Expressive/academic roles

The head of department's roles in this area proved to be the
most problematical for interviewees. Only the first two of
the activities mentioned below did heads of department claim
to perform with any degree of success:

a) holding departmental meeting

and

b) consultation with colleagues.

There was no opportunity to prove either the quality of the
departmental meetings, the management skills displayed by
heads of department or the quality of consultative procedures, but the impression gained from some interviewees was
that consultation was pitched at the level of a 'chat with a
colleague'. The quotation that: 'There's nothing much to
discuss about the work of the department ... the only thing
to worry about is the admin.' suggested that for some heads
of department the quality of departmental meetings may not be

too high.

c) Control and management of departmental staff

When this subject was discussed, interviewees displayed a range of apologetic attitudes, not wishing to offend their departmental colleagues by unprofessional behaviour.

It seemed that the concept 'professional' was interpreted in the minds of teachers as having the competence to teach, and an entitlement to autonomy. The classroom was thought to be the teacher's 'castle' vis-a-vis middle management control of staff. On the subject of supervising the methodology of teaching, the following responses are recorded to illustrate their attitude.

> I can trust my staff ... after all they are
> professional - that's what they are paid for; to do a
> professional job!

or:

> I would have to take a lead if my staff were
> inexperienced ...

a statement made to justify the status quo of non-interference or control of staff.

d) Checking on the quality of staff teaching

On this topic interviewees communicated high aspirations but theory and expectations were not translated into practice.

> One thing I would like to do ... I would like to go in
> to see my colleagues teach ... trip into the cupboard
> at the back of the room ... but it would be essential
> that they should also come to see me teach as part of
> the deal.

44

## Emerging Issues

Why was this not happening? Why the secrecy and embarrassment (tripping into the cupboard) in supervising the pace of teaching or appraising departmental staff competence? Why 'the deal'?

> If I had been evaluated by someone, I'm sure that I would then be prepared to evaluate others ... but there's the problem of time - there's just not enough time to do what I would like to do ... I suppose setting an example is not sufficiently forceful enough.

Another head of department thought that '... the department ought to evaluate itself'.

These random comments by interviewees suggested confusion, frustration, a lack of direction and confidence. Certainly, these issues were uncomfortable ones for heads of department.

### e) Delegation of tasks

The reluctance to manage staff affected the process and practice of delegation. For example,

> I wait for them (departmental members) to say: 'How about me doing something to help out' ... then I know that they are capable of taking things on.

Another stance of heads of department may be illustrated by the quotation 'I feel dubious about passing things on ... that's what I'm paid for'.

Such an attitude created a position of isolation, even though a head of department might have confidence in departmental members. Further evidence of non-delegation was: 'I'm not successful at getting other people involved with departmental work ... here is the syllabus, you teach the way you know best ...' which may be interpreted as abdication of management responsibilities. Another comment highlights their attitude towards delegation and the creation of an isolationist position: 'I tend to keep things to myself ... there are things I never tell anyone else about ... there are disadvantages in this ...' However, such an attitude ran counter to their desire to lead strong teams of teachers. There was little evidence of ways in which a departmental team was given the opportunity to develop as a team, other than the head of department giving members encouragement in routine matters.

### f) Managing probationary teachers

Work with probationary teachers was experienced by most interviewees in the pilot study. This role was often thought to be onerous, as reflected in the comment: 'I'm constantly having probationers ... not easy to settle people in ... nobody has trained me to do this. 'Who should be responsible for such training? Why had the head of department not been trained? Answers to such rhetorical questions were further possible lines of enquiry in an ensuing study.

Two telling remarks made by interviewees confirmed that there was much valuable research work to be done on the role of middle managers in secondary schools.

> As a middle manager we are squeezed from both sides ... it's rather uncomfortable

and

> I end up with a picture of frustration. We (H.o.D.'s) ought to have simulations on dealing with people ... especially the hard cases.

The discovery of answers to only some of these issues could contribute towards an improved efficiency and effectiveness of heads of department, which in turn could affect the quality of education offered to students in schools.

# Emerging Issues

Having used Taylor's Quadrant Model as a means of sifting data, I progressed with an analysis by focussing on two specific areas:

   1) Assumptions made by heads of department

   11) Paradoxes presented by heads of department

## Assumptions made by heads of department

 a) Teachers are professionals

Some assumptions were actually recognized by heads of department in their interviews, for example, that departmental members were professional which meant 'that they were competent and knew what they were doing'. Being a qualified teachers seemed to infer that a person was professional and should exercise autonomy. In practise this would probably lead to a position of isolation for many teachers. The concept of training, re-training, evaluation of work and staff appraisal seemed not to be acceptable bed-fellows with the concept of professional. In addition it was noted that 'being professional' was the god of success. By definition it was thought that professional teachers should not fail in their practice and therefore not readily discuss any failure which did occur. These particular attitudes are important to note in the process of a qualitative piece of research, and for planning training for heads of department.

 b) Heads of departments' understanding of management
    practice  - Innovation

The skills of planning a range of tasks from those matters financial to curriculum development, pre-supposed a head of department's understanding of the philosophy and implications of the subjects under consideration. One example, to highlight this assumption, was the lack of understanding about the concept and implications of innovation. From the work of

## Emerging Issues

Hoyle it is clear that innovation 'depends upon changing people and providing means of improving receptivity to change'. (Hoyle, 1970) The practice of innovation is a complex organizational exercise requiring the skills of planning, organizing, directing, controlling, co-ordinating and evaluating, and will also include negotiating matters with colleagues. Many heads of department viewed innovation as an exercise of 'try and see whether it works', which may be a major reason for a number of interviewees remarking that 'a lot of time is spent planning for things that do not happen'.

### c) Head of department as co-ordinator

An assumption was made about the role of heads of department as co-ordinators of activities; indeed the philosophical argument that a department by definition was any number of persons greater than one, pre-supposes a co-ordinating role for a head of department. From the data collection, a per-ceived minimal activity of negotiation, delegator and staff appraisal suggested that the co-ordinating role was not effective.

### d) A static model

In dialogue about their departments, heads of department invariably assumed a static model of their department's work, as opposed to the reality of a dynamic model. Reviews, evaluation and INSET were not given high priority and, in many cases, avoided. Leadership was another concept which was thought of as static, with the leader almost always thought of as being at the front of the phalanx. (See also Howson and Woolnough, 1982)

### Paradoxes presented by heads of department

#### a) Team building

Mention has already been made about the desire of heads of

# Emerging Issues

department to build strong departmental teams, yet there was a reluctance to co-ordinate, delegate, negotiate and evaluate staff performance.

b) Staff appraisal

The use of time has already been highlighted, the desire of heads of department to appraise departmental members but not having enough time to do so. This raised the question of their priority of tasks and their degree of commitment to be middle managers.

c) Evaluation

The desire to evaluate a department: 'I would like to do this ...', then the response 'How do you do it?' puts into sharp focus the need for training, the fear of sharing failure and shortcomings.

d) Personnel management

An ironic situation was declared by heads of department who wished to give their staff job satisfaction, but they appeared to make no positive plans to ascertain staff needs or seek to raise staff morale.

e) Management of change

Managing change seemed to be abhorent to the majority of heads of department interviewed in the pilot study, yet change was welcomed by them in innovating curriculum development.

f) Insularity of departments

A final observation was the comparative isolation of most departments within schools caused by the insular attitude of many members of the teaching profession, yet curriculum development often required an integration of departments.

## Emerging Issues

Reluctance to liaise with peer group middle managers raised a range of considerations about the quality of education offered to students.

Reflecting upon the view that a department is a unit of the whole school, and the work of those units should be greater than the sum of the whole, one may question the effectiveness of senior management in co-ordinating the roles of middle management in schools. During the course of these interviews and the subsequent analysis of the data many questions formulated in the mind of the researcher such as:

  (i) Do heads of department lack administrative skills?

 (ii) Do heads of department have an unrealistic teaching load?

(iii) How much role conflict is built into the role of a head of department?

 (iv) Is training in the management of time a need of most heads of department?

  (v) What is the most critical need of heads of department?

Many other questions remained in the forefront of my mind and the knowledge that the analysis of the pilot study data had re-inforced previous research findings. In particular the expressive roles of heads of department presented the major problems for them, and, therefore, I thought that an extended study of the role of heads of department in a school would create the opportunity to refine these apparent problems and shed some light in solving some of them.

# 4 INSIGHT INTO A TYPICAL SCHOOL

The following criteria dictated the choice of a school in which to carry out an in-depth study.

1. In most L.E.A.'s the majority of secondary schools were comprehensive, and educational literature, including the Black Papers (Cox and Boyson, 1977) suggested that curriculum development and curriculum innovation had been most marked in this type of school. It was therefore assumed that in this type of school heads of department were likely to be pro-active in the role as middle managers.

2. A school should be large enough to ensure that a full range of subject departments were available for the purpose of data collection: implicit in the size of the school roll was the size of every department. It was thought that middle managers in this study should have at least one other person in his department.

3. To avoid any preconceived judgements on my part, a school should be selected outside the L.E.A. in which I worked.

4. A school which practised an organic style of

51

## Insight into a Typical School

management was sought in the belief that the
mechanistic style (Burns and Stalker, 1968)
would limit the scope and skills of middle
managers; whereas an organic style might highlight
the interpersonal and management skills of heads
of department, not least their willingness in a
non-hierarchical orientated organization, to be
frank and open.

5.  Continuity of service within a school, especially
    amongst middle managers, would ensure that the
    latter had enjoyed the opportunity to develop their
    respective skills over a period and establish their
    roles.

I believed that the selection of a school based on the  above
criteria would create an arena of good practice as opposed to
mediocre professional practice.

Hodson High School was  selected from a number of possible
schools which fulfilled the five criteria detailed above. For
this I had approached officers from my  own L.E.A.,  seeking
recommendations  of  schools  where they considered that good
middle management practice may be found. Hodson  High  School
was  considered  by  a number of professional persons to be a
lively and forward looking organization where many aspects of
curriculum development were worthy of note.  One  description
was  that  'Hodson High School had a lively staff where there
were a lot of good things  happening'.  Another  person  commented  that  'It  is a school in which much thought has been
given to the organization and development of the  process  of
learning'.

## Negotiating a contract

Bearing in mind the words of George Homans:

The final emphasis must always be on the group (in

52

this case - heads of department) before us. Lord
Nelson, greatest of all admirals, after explaining to
his captains the plan of attack he intended to use at
the battle of Trafalgar, went on to say, 'No captain
can do very wrong who places his ship alongside that
of the enemy'. In the same way, no one studying a
group will go far wrong if he gets close to it, and by
whatever methods are available observes all that he
can. Nothing that can illuminate the group should be
ruled out for doctrinaire reasons. We shall be blind
enough without wilfully narrowing our vision. (Homans,
1950)

I sought to negotiate a situation in which I might get alongside heads of department to observe all possible perspectives
of their role.

The major task in the initial interview with the headteacher
of Hodson High School was to explain the rationale of an ethnographic study; that it is based on the assumption that what
people say and do is consciously and unconsciously shaped by
the social situation in which they work. The headteacher was
a scientist, and the question of validity and reliability of
qualitative work became a focus of attention. To him a researcher without a precise hypothesis was viewed with
suspicion; as a ship without a rudder, and the process of
qualitative research methodology had to be explained in
detail. (See Hamilton, 1977; Hammersley and Atkinson, 1983;
Woods, 1986) However, it is significant to record that a
description of the historical background of head of department's role, an analysis of previous research proved to be
helpful in giving the proposed research programme credibility.

Even at this early stage of negotiation, data collection
about Hodson High School had begun, as the headteacher gave
his views on the type of school he had developed during the
past eight years. After further discussion we decided that he

would present to a senior staff meeting (deputies and heads of department) a summary of this initial discussion and gain a response about the proposed study taking place two terms hence. There was a lively exchange of views about the re-search proposals and anxiety was expressed about a researcher being present in the school for such a long period.

Fear was also expressed that a researcher might take on an inspectorial role. The fate of the data collected was questioned. There was anxiety about the possible involvement of the L.E.A. Confidentiality and anonymity were obviously uppermost in their minds 'Could the L.E.A. demand a report from the researcher and then use the data as a stick to beat us with?' was a query, and also, 'How much time would we have to give to this chap as he could waste a great deal of our time' was another question. Finally a decision was made to meet me at the next senior staff meeting to discover more about a proposed 'fly on the wall' approach and whether it was thought that I could be trusted.

The above reactions are not uncommon amongst teachers who value their professional autonomy, and who are also sensitive to such issues as accountability and staff appraisal. The minutes of the next senior staff meeting described me as a 'guest' and introduced by the headteacher as one who would like to be a 'fly on the wall' in order to see how middle managers functioned in the school. I stressed that the re-search would, I hoped, have a practical use in assisting the process of INSET and the professional development of staff beyond the bounds of Hodson High School. As previously agreed with the headteacher, after this session of questions and answers I withdrew from the meeting to enable the staff to have a frank discussion about my possible access to the school.

On reflection, if, at this stage of negotiating access to the school, a clear recognizable hypothesis or specific problem could have been advanced, my position with heads of de-partment would have been more comfortable. The explanation of

# Insight into a Typical School

the proposed work, and in particular the validity of qualitative research methodology would have been less of a problem for them to grasp. The minutes of this senior staff meeting, which came to hand after a contract had been negotiated, showed that a whole spectrum of views had been expressed after I had left them. One nagging fear, however, remained paramount: that the L.E.A. might claim the research data. The headteacher agreed not to communicate formally in the first instance with the Chief Education Officer, but to approach the Area Education Officer. In this way, the approach to the L.E.A. would be exploratory. A verbal exchange between the officer and the headteacher satisfied both people and was followed by a formal letter from the latter. The only other area of concern to the staff was my ensuring that sources of data remained anonymous.

## The School - Ethos, Organization and Philosophy

Hodson High School is situated in a semi-rural area, and its one thousand two hundred students came from the main centres of population as well as from many small villages. The local authority developed various means of encouraging employment opportunities by attracting industry to the area. This, in turn, caused the local council to create a policy of housing for essential employees, and the industrial growth supplemented the areas of traditional economic dependence on agriculture. Frankton, where the High School was built in 1975, had in excess of one hundred companies on the town's indusrial estate, with a range of industries from light and heavy engineering on the one hand, and the manufacture of pharmaceuticals on the other.

The intake of Hodson High School was a comprehensive mix of students from the outlying villages, from the new town development areas as well as the indigenous population of Frankton. The town's recreational and cultural facilities, and a Sports Hall and Squash Courts were constructed on the school campus for the dual use of the school and local community, and the school was committed to a policy of close liaison with the community. There was a flourishing Adult Centre in which about half of the school staff were involved in various capacities. A pre-school playgroup on site and a Saturday morning Music and Drama Centre are examples of the school playing host to community activities. It was also noted that there was a very good professional liaison with feeder schools.

Hodson High School had a two tier curriculum organization with a framework of eight major curriculum areas - English, Expressive Arts, Creative Arts, Humanities, Mathematics, Modern Languages, Physical Education and Science, every one with a faculty head. Faculty heads received Burnham Scale IV posts and were responsible for the overall organization, policy and financing of their faculty, within which were individual subjects or courses organized by heads of department on Burnham Scale IV award. The fact that these teachers were middle managers and on a par with heads of faculty accounted for their initial inclusion in the study. Amongst the twelve hundred students, the open-access sixth form numbered one hundred and forty students, offering a range of both two and one year courses.

The school's senior management team (S.M.T.) consisted of headteacher, two deputies and three senior teachers. Members of staff on Scale IV with the S.M.T. formed the Senior Staff Committee. All heads of department including those on Burnham scales below scale IV were encouraged to hold departmental meetings and to consult with colleagues, thus reflecting a consultative and organic style of management projected by the headteacher. All but four of the original twenty three heads of department appointed at the inauguration of the school were in post at that time. Suites of rooms for every faculty enhanced the working environment of departments.

Hodson High School had its own peculiarities which may be judged 'disadvantages' in a school's organization. When the school opened with its first cohort of students, the first

# Insight into a Typical School

flush of staff appointments were middle managers followed by scale I's and occasionally scale II's in the ensuing years. Amongst the scale I teachers were many probationary teachers and this skew in the staffing was such at the time of the study. The headteacher referred to this peculiarity in an internal document:

> It is somewhat ironical that only a few months after
> an inspector had observed the relative youth of our
> staff - 'committed and enthusiastic but inexperienced'
> - I have had to contend with a turnover of 14
> relatively junior staff leading to the appointment,
> yet again, of 10 probationary teachers ...
> Fortunately, we have been able to obtain some very
> good new teachers, but the problems of inexperience
> continue to show up and remain the greatest single
> preoccupation of both senior staff and heads of
> department.

However the headteacher continued in another document

> ... but I do not regard the problem of inexperience as
> cause for gloom. It is extremely stimulating to work
> with a young and enthusiastic staff. It seems to me to
> be the right way round, and the situation can only get
> better as experience develops, provided the structure
> is there to underpin it.

The opportunity for heads of department to be involved in the management of the school was apparent from the above quotations, and heads of department were presented with the challenge of moulding their departmental team without a great deal of interference from senior colleagues. It was the considered view of all members of the S.M.T. that 'Heads of department have developed their own individual styles', and this observation was particularly noteworthy as the philosophy of the school was that a liberal attitude should prevail in all its activities.

## Insight into a Typical School

Amongst the heads of department there were only two who had held middle management posts prior to their appointments to Hodson High School, but these were for small departments. The stability of the middle management staffing during the past eight years had presented the S.M.T. with the opportunity to observe their professional development over a period of time. This was particulartly pertinent as the majority of the staff on taking up their appointments were inexperienced in fulfilling head of department roles.

Throughout its short history, it was generally agreed amongst heads of department that 'an atmosphere of co-operation, friendliness, consultation and altogether a positive attitude persisted' at Hodson High School. One head of department who at the time of the research was about to leave said: 'There is a sense of purpose and dedication of the staff which I haven't found in any other school I have worked in'. Another middle manager remarked: 'I'm much happier at this school than the last ... you're allowed to get on here ...'.

In conclusion, quotations about Hodson High School from the observations of an independent professional source stated:

> A high proportion of the staff are graduates and the majority of the teaching is done by specialists. Many of the achievements of the school are properly attributable to the personal qualities of these teachers .... Teaching is conscientiosly undertaken, and many staff give freely of their time to conduct extra-curricular activities. These all play an important part in establishing pupil/staff relationships, most of which are very good.

The vibrance of the staff was apparent in the common room where lively exchanges of view frequently took place; an 'openness' which was noted by visitors. Such a set of circumstances presented an ideal environment for the study to take place.

# 5 AN ETHNOGRAPHIC STUDY

## Introduction

The process of this research was to refine progressively the steps of the work, sifting and selecting. It is significant to record that the impact of the training needs of heads of department was not registered by me until mid-way through phase three of the research. Putting this fact into a time sequence, the decision to focus on the perceptions of their training needs was not taken until three months after the data collection at Hodson High School had begun. At this stage of decision taking, the data from phase one and two were further revised in the light of that decision.

Data collected from interviews throughout the study were transcribed and analysed at the end of every individual session, and the corporate data bank of each phase was carefully analysed and considered prior to determining a strategy of approach for the next phase. In total, I recorded over one hundred and fifty hours of taped interviews, and had some seven hundred hours of dialogue with the staff of Hodson High School.

In order to preserve the anonymity and confidentiality of all interviewees the procedures used both in analysing data

## An Ethnographic Study

and in writing the study were:

1. Teachers were given a number and fictitious name

2. All genders were designated first person masculine

3. Venues were always noted as 'classroom' regardless of whether in reality it was a laboratory, workshop or classroom.

## Phase One: Unstructured Interviews with Heads of Department and Senior Management

In this first phase of the study, twenty nine unstructured interviews involving four members of the senior management team, six pastoral heads, eight heads of department scale IV and eleven heads of department scale III took place. Apart from the senior management team members, all were all asked for similar information, namely:

'Tell me about your experience since working at the school',

'Tell me what you do'.

The other four interviewees were asked a different second question

'Tell me about your work with middle managers'.

The procedures for interviewing members of staff and analysing the data obtained took exactly the same form as that used in the Pilot Study described in the previous chapter.

## The first question

The first - 'Tell me about your experience of working at Hodson High School!' - was designed to give an historical

perspective of the growth of the school; to assist him in
putting comments and events into context, and to give interviewees an opportunity to discuss how they perceived that
they had changed over a period of time.

> We were a young staff ... and thought that nothing but
> good could come out of the situation. The staff were
> dynamic, enthusiastic, encouraging, innovative ... but
> there was a lack of experience which caused many
> problems.

Eight years on from the inauguration of Hodson High School,
heads of department having said, 'The experience of working
here ... I wouldn't have missed it for the world', found that
with falling student rolls, the chances of teacher promotion
was minimized. From the perspective of members of the senior
management team

> Heads of department have gradually grown into their
> various jobs but are now jaded, and some desperately
> looking for new openings and ways of finding a new
> lease of life

> A number of heads of department are getting burnt out
> ... I don't know what the answer is to keep them
> vibrant until some of them obtain other posts.

These views reinforced the difficulties experienced by heads
of department such as: 'Where do we go from here ... ? - we
need to rethink how middle management can gain personal
development without leaving the school.'

Such comments alerted me to consider ways in which such a
desire might become a reality, as the log jam in the teaching
profession regarding promotion was a national problem, not
limited to Hodson High School. One head of department made
the comment: 'I dispair - I'm horrified - I am on job
application number sixty four' which reinforces the point.
The experience of the middle managers at Hodson High School

were similar to those of their peers in the pilot study, although the frustration and cynicism was expressed more forcefully.

## The second question

In analysing the second - Tell me what you do', Taylor's quadrant model, described in Chapter One, was used again, since this had proved to be an effective method of initially sifting the data collected in the pilot study. The topics listed on the Analyis Sheets were raised by interviewees, not imposed by me. However, any significant omissions were noted at the completion of the interviews. The six pastoral heads were included at the beginning of the study, because they were considered to be middle managers as well as heads of subject departments and they could well form a significant part of the study. This view was reinforced in an H.M.I. document, "Departmental Organisation in Secondary Schools", which suggested that

> The creation of posts such as head of section, head of
> house and year tutor ... has to some extent reduced
> the status and influence of heads of department.
> (Welsh Office, 1984)

Throughout the first phase of the study thought was given to the perceived major problem areas acknowledged by heads of department, as well as those aspects of their role which were not perceived to be problematic but considered to be so by me. In addition, consideration was given to the paradoxes recorded from the data and also assumptions interviewees made when describing their role.

## Major Problems of Heads of Department

The major problems experienced by heads of department in seeking to fulfil their roles were the expressive or

62

person-centred roles. This finding confirmed the results of previous research (for example, Lambert, 1972; Howson, 1980 and Archer, 1981) and the pilot study completed prior to starting this study. In contrast, the instrumental or task-centred roles proved to be less problematical and they were confident in fulfilling such roles, apart from some administrative responsibilities.

The limited amount of time available for heads of department to perform their various roles was claimed to be an unreasonable constraint, and it was apparent that potential role conflict was built into their role. They were expected to be both master teachers and middle managers, although many heads of department preferred the phrase 'administrator' rather than 'manager'. A conflict of loyalty to headteacher and to departmental members was also noted; a consequence of being a 'middle' manager. 'A major problem is where my loyalty lies ... up or down ... If I tell the Head I would be sneaky ... it's difficult being an in-betweener.' It was no surprise that work with probationary teachers was frequently mentioned in interviews, for, since its inauguration, Hodson High School has constantly had large numbers of probationers. Suspicion about this work was aroused in my mind when it was said by an interviewee:

> Our probationer this year is high calibre ... no problem ... needs a little help now and again, but in general, things hang together of their own accord.

Such suspicion about the management of probationary teachers was further justified on hearing the remark by a member of the senior management team.

> We have had as many as sixteen probationers at a time ... it's the head of department's responsibility to manage the induction ... it has been discussed with them, and mostly they have not moved.

Sifting out comments and reactions related to training, it

was clear to me that the majority of heads of department believed they were not trained for the tasks of middle
management. '... being a good classroom teacher doesn't make
you a good head of department ...' suggested that there must
be skills and techniques which heads of department regarded
as necessary for their effective role performance. Another
quotation from an interviewee who was experiencing a range of
problems caused 'alarm bells' to ring in my mind:

> ... people think you do these things (management
> practices) by instinct as opposed to being trained to
> be a head of department ... When you are made head of
> department ... it's like being put into a rowing boat
> without any oars ... very little advice on how to run
> a department ... it's assumed having taught for a
> number of years you would know how to run a
> department.

A final example of an indicator amongst many others which
gave force to the decision to pursue the subject of training
came from an experienced head of department when he simply
said: 'I need training as a middle manager ... middle
managers ought to be worth their salt.'

## Paradoxes

There were three significant paradoxes in phase one of the
study. First, that all heads of department desired and worked
towards building a strong departmental team, yet, negotiations with and delegation of tasks to departmental members
remained weak and were apparently often non-existent skills.
It seemed ironic that many departmental members were not
given the opportunity to play active roles as team members
other than the role of a classroom teacher.

Secondly, there was a desire on the part of heads of department to make innovations in order to generate a vibrant
organization, yet time and again, the result of these

innovative activities was to cause the opposite effect, namely, frustration amongst departmental members.

The third paradox was that heads of department displayed the confidence that 'I'm sure that I know where I am going', and, 'I'm on the right lines', but modes of evaluation were rarely practised as there '... wasn't enough time ...'

These three paradoxes presented me with specific areas of exploration, seeking to discover the reasons why heads of department experienced such difficulties in these management practices.

## Assumptions

One major assumption made by heads of department about members of staff was that a qualified teacher was a 'professional'. The term 'professional' was a portmanteau-type phrase which was used to assume that a teacher was competent in classroom management; could be trusted with confidence; had a large degree of independence and autonomy. It was implied that this made the leadership of a department more difficult to operate than if teachers were not professionals. Frequently heads of department requested tasks to be done as a 'favour' rather than a legitimate professional delegated task.

Professionalism often created isolation, as it was generally assumed that heads of department would not share difficulties with each other, and that not being able to cope with a problem would be considered by the peer group and senior staff as a stigma of failure. To monitor the progress of students taught by a colleague was thought to be an embarrassing activity: 'It was much easier to have a quick look at a pile of books at the back of a classroom than to sit in on a lesson ...'.

Often it was assumed that, 'All was going well' until a

## An Ethnographic Study

complaint was made by a parent, student or colleague. In other words, there was little, if any, evaluation or appraisal practised, and heads of department relied on a sixth sense to gauge the quality of the work of their departments.

## Decisions

At the conclusion of the first phase of the study a decision was taken to limit the scope of the study to the investigation of expressive roles of heads of department, that is, people-related roles. Heads of department were particularly sensitive about the problems they experienced in dealing with people and this had been given scant attention by previous researchers although noted as a problematic area for heads of department. It was with comparative ease that instrumental tasks were accomplished, apart from the limited time available in which to complete such responsibilities. Another decision was not to pursue the middle management role of year heads. Although like the subject head of department their role was evolving, it was clear from observation and interview that tutor teams were transitory. Furthermore, members of staff considered that they had been appointed to the school staff to teach a subject on the curriculum and were not primarily appointed to be a form tutor. These factors compounded the problems related to the role of the year head as a middle manager and it was judged that this particular role justified a separate study in its own right.

## Phase Two - Daily Observation of Heads of Department

The next logical step in this study was to match what head of department interviewees claimed to do with what they actually achieved. I laid plans to shadow them during the course of their day-to-day work, except for observing them teach. Consideration was given to asking heads of department to keep

66

a daily diary over a period of time, but obviously if they complied with such a request they would use valuable time recording data rather than proceeding with a 'normal' day's work. Furthermore, with nineteen heads of department recording these activities there would be a range of interpretations of perceived activities as well as a variation in the quality of recording data. Indeed, their relative value judgements would invalidate the process of triangulation.

I decided on three objectives:

1) to match what heads of department claimed to do with what they actually achieved

2) to observe the effectiveness of their work

3) to note the assumptions which teachers made in their demands of heads of department.

I adopted the role of participant observer throughout the course of the study; the 'shadowing' of heads of department during this phase of the study throughout the day would possibly give a further dimension to the role of head of department or would confirm what otherwise would be gained in a piecemeal way. To obtain a sense of continuity of a head of department's work I considered it advantageous to shadow any one person for two consecutive days, giving an opportunity to compare and contrast any one day with another.

Knowing that heads of department taught on average for eighty per cent of a school week and that they would not be observed during that teaching time, this exercise could become time-consuming with little value. Because of this, Phase two of the study was limited to two school weeks - ten working days. Five heads of department, therefore, had to be selected and terms of reference negotiated with them. I was keen to see the most ideal conditions under which heads of department worked in order to observe possibly quality management practices and to choose heads of department who represented a

## An Ethnographic Study

broad spectrum of the school's curriculum.

The five most experienced heads of department from Creative
Crafts, English, Humanities, Modern Languages and Science
were selected and I 'shadowed' each of them from their time
of arrival on the school campus until their time of departure
at the end of the school day. Notes were made on such
subjects as the use of a head of department's time, people he
met, planned and unplanned meetings, decisions taken during
the day, his relationship with colleagues and the management
practices exercised.

## Significant Factors

During this time I observed a range of head of department
practices, including the chairmanship of departmental meetings, the writing of a probationary teacher's report, the
deployment of staff for the forthcoming academic year and
dealings with situations which went 'wrong' resulting in a
flurry of activity. Added dimensions were gained to the data
collected in phase one, such as the fact that most heads of
department found dificulty in delegation which, if it had
been effective, would have aided the process of team building
and the staff development of their departmental members.

> So often when you delegate, different people have
> different priorities to me and you assume that they
> see things as you do ... you also assume that they
> have the ability to organize these things.

A great deal of departmental business was observed taking
place in school corridors, with most outspoken comments about
a range of topics in the privacy of the cloakroom. I also
noted that whilst focussing on the expressive roles of heads
of department I became aware that most instrumental tasks
were effectively accomplished. The fact that heads of
department frequently allowed themselves to be over-burdened
with day-to-day minutiae, caused a question to arise in my

# An Ethnographic Study

mind; to what extent do heads of department avoid their expressive role? Many other questions were raised from what heads of department said and did during their day-to-day work such as why do they find the practice of delegation so difficult, and what is their most difficult problem?

During phase two many problems besetting heads of department were highlighted. At the conclusion of this phase it was apparent that most heads of department lacked interpersonal skills. I noticed that they cared about members of their staff, and as one person said at the end of a day's observation:

> ... you will have noticed that I have spoken with
> every member of my department today ... I like to do
> this and ensure that everybody is happy ...

but this concern was categorized as superficial 'staff welfare'. In the opinion of another head of department many of his peer group lacked managerial skills. 'My colleagues often fall down in controlling people ...', which highlighted the main problems: controlling, and co-ordinating the work of the department. Following an exchange of views between a head of department and a departmental member the former remarkd to me:

> They talk about accountabilities ... and being told
> when things are not going well ... but when you do,
> they get upset and say that it is not fair ...

The expressive roles of a head of department were numerous and demanding, involving the practice of many skills and techniques. However, based on an analysis of phases one and two, the key areas which were frequently coming to the fore in their minds were appraisal, delegation, evaluation and innovation. It was also noted that often heads of department arrived late for lessons as they had been engaged in discussion about 'important business' whilst en route to their class. It was also recorded that:

> ... you have frequently to slot in admin. work whilst
> officially teaching, otherwise deadlines could not be
> met ... I guess if my teaching load had not been light
> today that it would have suffered with these wretched
> lists to complete ...

With this and other collaborative evidence, the management of
time was thought to be another key area to pursue in phase
three of the study, when departmental members would be interviewed, giving an added depth and another perspective to the
understanding of the role of heads of department.

## Phase Three - Unstructured Interviews with Departmental Members

### Introduction

At the conclusion of phase two, five major areas of concern
had been expressed by heads of department:

a) Delegation;
b) Evaluation;
c) Innovation;
d) Management of Time;
e) Staff Appraisal.

It was then decided to ascertain whether departmental members
expressed similar concerns as their head of department, or if
they had other areas of concern.

Forty two unstructured interviews were taped, some lasting
for thirty five minutes, others as long as sixty five
minutes, which involved members from the same five faculties
as those heads of department 'shadowed' in phase two, namely
the faculties of English, Expressive Crafts, Humanities,
Modern Languages and Science. The members of staff who were

interviewed may be put into the following categories:

a) Full-time members of department
b) Part-time members teaching in more than one department
c) Senior members of staff having a major role elsewhere in the school
d) Supply teachers filling temporary vacancies.

Every interviewee was asked one question:

> What support did you expect when you joined the department?

which was designed to be non-threatening, but to elucidate the perceived role of a head of department.

It was interesting that in all cases 'the expectations of the departmental support' was personalized in the role of the head of department. Forty five different topics were raised by interviewees and were recorded on analysis sheets, but only the expressive roles were considered in the actual data analysis. Some of the topics were facets of the major topics logged at the conclusion of phase two; for example, 'showing empathy', 'constructive criticism' and 'counselling staff on professional development', were all considered for the purposes of this study to be an integral part of staff appraisal. This approach created coherent topics from the rich but fragmented data collected, thus making the analysis of the data more manageable. However, skills such as prioritizing and other facets of major topics such as the skills of planning were not ignored.

## Significant factors

Departmental members identified three broad areas of management for which they believed heads of department were responsible:

## An Ethnographic Study

a) The control of teacher behaviour and professional practice within a department.

b) The support of 'professional activities' in the classroom.

c) The motivation of colleagues, ensuring that skills and talents of individual teachers were maximized for the common good of students and staff.

The majority of interviewees acknowledged that

> The most difficult thing (within the role of a (H.o.D.) is staff ... important thing is to try to maintain standards and improve motivation and co-operation.

Departmental members' views incorporated four of the five main topics listed above, that is, delegation, evaluation, innovation and staff development. Time management was not raised as a major issue, possibly because of the nature of the question - 'What support did you expect when you joined the department? - However, in their responses department staff assumed that heads of department were able to manage time in order to achieve the role they expected of them, and two further topics came to the fore, that of team work and negotiation. Team work had already been noted in phase one of the study as a potential topic for further investigation, and in this third phase, teachers expressed very strongly that they wished to identify themselves with their departmental team and expected their respective head of department to integrate them into the department's work. The other new topic, negotiation, came to the fore following an interview with a departmental member who was also a teacher's union representative. It was he who shared his experience of attending a union course in order to learn how to negotiate with his employers. He thought that heads of department would be more effective in dealing with their colleagues if they learnt the skills of negotiating, and would thereby be clearer in their minds as to what they wished to achieve.

> In any case, negotiation would free them (heads of department) to actually sit down and discuss matters with us ... it would have certainly slowed down the number of innovations we have had to cope with ...

The focus of that person's argument caused me to review the data already collected in phase three and in the previous two phases, and I found the lack of negotiation a marked phenomenon. Departmental members also commented that some senior staff and heads of department, in their view, needed training to compensate for what they perceived as weaknesses in their role performance. In the case of heads of department it was suggested that:

> They need a probationary period ... and an idiot's guide to surviving your first year as a head of department would be a useful aid ... and this (the above suggestion) would also assist senior staff in helping heads of department to identify areas of weakness.

The problem of supporting heads of department remained an unsolved problem for some interviewees and to quote a perceptive member of staff:

> Such matters will only begin to be resolved as they are brought out into the open and discussed in a professional way by all parties concerned.

Staff development remained a powerful instrument in the minds of all staff in order to gain promotion and improve career prospects. However, there were signs that many departmental members also thought staff development was an essential part of professional development in order to gain job satisfaction.

members, heads of department and senior management - were in agreement, that heads of department required training to cope with their expressive roles. I had listed in my fieldwork diary many skills and managerial practices under the heading 'important issues', such as the skills of chairmanship and prioritizing, but the major broad topics of concern proved to be staff appraisal, delegation, evaluation, innovation, negotiation, team building and the management of time. Each of these topics could form an individual study, and in practice would involve the mastering of many management skills. It was my intention, having identified these areas of concern, to continue to probe more into them and seek to discover more fully the extent of the gulf between heads of department intent and practice.

## Phase Four - Semi-structured Interviews with Heads of Department

### Introduction

Having now identified seven areas of the head of department's role where incumbents experienced major difficulties and would desire training, it was important that at no time should the subject of training needs be communicated to them. If training needs of heads of department was declared as a major interest, it would be inevitable that interviewees would respond with data they perceived I required. To probe more deeply into these identified areas it was necessary to introduce semi-structured focussed interviews as opposed to un-structured interviews used in the previous phases. The focussed interview gave parameters of discussion and the opportunity to probe significant data already raised by interviewees.

Re-analysing the phase one data in the light of the development of phase two and three, statements declaring difficulties experienced by heads of department in the major areas identified to be pursued, staff appraisal, delegation, evaluation, innovation, negotiation, team building and time management were listed. From a long list of statements I chose those which represented the views of the great majority of heads of department; and this was further pruned since there was much duplication of topic material. It was important to have a blend of precise and open-ended statements culled from the data to conceal from the interviewees the specific reasons for mounting this next phase of the study.

In compiling a short list of statements, I was conscious of the weight of evidence related to the role conflict experienced by heads of department. This specific concern remained in the forefront of my mind; further evidence gained would add to the context in which training needs of heads of department could be considered. The number of statements was eventually limited to seven to enable heads of department to discuss them at some depth within an hour interview. These statements were typed on a sheet of paper with a prefacing comment to heads of department designed to maintain professional co-operation with them which up to this time had been of a very high order. They gave freely of their time and expressed their opinions and feelings in a frank and open manner.

Wishing to limit any pressure which may be unconsciously placed on interviewees, I made this document a confidential paper; no statement would be disclosed to senior or departmental members. It was also decided that each head of department should have the "Comments Sheet" at least twenty four hours before an interview took place to give time for considered views to be expressed. Interviewees also had the option of choosing the order in which they responded to comments.

## Statement One

I have grown into the job (H.o.D.) ... I was relatively

green when I came here.

The reason for including this first statement was to identify those heads of department who considered that they were prepared, and/or who had received training for their posts prior to appointment. I also wanted to discover whether they considered that they had learned new skills during their present period of office, and to identify managerial skills which were considered essential for all heads of department. From such data the training needs of heads of department would be put into sharp focus.

The majority of heads of department freely acknowledged that they were unprepared on taking up post to accept fully the role of a head of department. 'Most of us were thrashing around in the dark' was one comment. Another response was:

> I had a false impression of what it was all about ... the job was harder than I had anticipated.

Another said

> True, nobody tells us what the role of the head of department is ... is it possible?

This latter comment reflected frustration and raised again the vagueness of the head of department role definition. It also questioned the nature of their middle management role, that heads of department found the role impossible to fulfil and experienced a lack of training. A final example of an initial response to this first statement was:

> I agree; I have grown into the job. I have had to adapt, but without any guidance.

Many other comments also suggested that guidance was required by heads of department interviewed but there was little forthcoming.

## An Ethnographic Study

It was established from answers to this first question that training was required by all heads of department apart from one person, and that the greatest concern and need for training was in managing people, appraising them and counselling them.

## Statement Two

Too much is expected of us ... what suffers is your teaching.

This statement was selected to probe the built-in role conflict of the head of department role, and also to discover more about his skills in managing time. A strong message had been given by interviewees that they believed that they were not coping adequately with their work load, and specific areas where they were not coping could be explored.

The role of master teacher was in direct conflict with managerial roles, and from choice the former role always took priority

We must keep in perspective that we (H.o.D.'s) are here to teach; hence you have to be a super organiser

... they (an unspecified authority) ought to divorce the head of department job from that of the classroom teacher ...

The topic of role conflict was critical to heads of department and will be pursued later.

The difficulties of time management was very much in evidence and this was so in previous phases of the study. However, after taking into consideration the tension of role conflict and the heavy teaching loads deployed to heads of department,

## Ethnographic Study

it was still clear that they needed to acquire skills in the management of time and this topic will be considered in a later chapter.

The frank approach of interviewees is demonstrated in the quotation below but is also one of many responses which reinforced my view that the training needs of heads of department was a realistic avenue to pursue.

> I'm jibbing about it (statement two) ... we have a few staff who still do not know what a job of work is ... things keep going wrong and we are too nice to one another ... we certainly need a proper training and need appraising ... what do they do in industry?

This quotation also raised the importance of staff appraisal, and caused heads of department to talk about evaluation, innovation and other management skills. However, the main thrust of concern was related to the importance of appropriate training to fulfil their role, the frustration and stress caused through role conflict and the problems of time management.

## Statement Three

> People think that we do these things by instinct as opposed to being trained to be a head of department.

Heads of department inferred or made direct statements that they needed management training; what would be their attitude to the suggestion of training? The quotation in statement three was presented to interviewees to ascertain how much training they had already received and the nature of the training. I also wished to determine the skills they considered they needed to be effective heads of department.

There was overwhelming support for regular INSET in order to develop successfully the role of heads of department.

## Ethnographic Study

'Definitely room for INSET because there's none' was one blunt reaction. Another interviewee confirmed the latter statement to his experience:

> True, you find out as you go along what you are
> supposed to do ... then find out how to do it. None of
> us have been trained to be a head of department
> ...setting up a team by instinct. Good personal
> relationships I need to establish ...

Following the concensus view amongst heads of department that INSET management training was lacking both at Hodson High School and within the L.E.A., one of many criticisms may be quoted.

> The L.E.A. should provide regular INSET, for example,
> the 'bread and butter' things ... organising and
> running a departmental meeting, delegation, causing
> good relationships with people and so on. Getting
> people to know their limits; getting them involved on
> creating a departmemtal team rather than people doing
> their own thing.

Another interviewee implied a criticism of the teaching profession, the Government and L.E.A.s:

> We are expected to set things up for ourselves ... in
> our absence (on a course) things are expected to go on
> ... when we come back from INSET we are not given the
> time or the facilities to set up anything we think is
> good.

In this case the interviewee was comparing his experience of working in industry with the facilities and resources available to him in his present occupation.

The overwhelming priority need shared with me was the skills to manage colleagues.

# Ethnographic Study

> One faculty is going to have six probationers ...
> nobody has ever taken us aside on how to deal with
> them. I had a probationer who had a nervous breakdown
> ... and it was said that I had put him under too much
> pressure and the finger was pointed at me ...

To emphasize this concern another head of department admitted:

> I cannot cope with managing people ... it is a matter
> of have a chat and do your best. How do you get the
> staff to do what you want ... by soft soaping them?
> ... Buying them a drink at the pub? ... To be
> diplomatic, or tell them off? There should be a system
> of how you deal with this sort of thing ... we work by
> hunch, not by training.

A series of specific management skills were noted which heads
of department considered that they lacked and these tallied
with those already designated in phases one to three. For
example,

> I would like pointers for doing things ... ways of
> changing things, dealing with crisis situations;
> informing members of staff of what they are doing is
> not particularly very good ... how to counsel adults
> ... these things are too important to be left to
> acquire as you go along ... you have the
> responsibility of a colleague's career ... that is a
> good reason for creating a good department and being
> able to manage it properly.

The collective thoughts, views and aspirations of heads of
department supported both the provision of a planned programme of training for those preparing for promotion to the
position of head of department, and for those actually holding such positions. Unfortunately frustration and insecurity
remained for the majority of departmental heads at Hudson

## Ethnographic Study

High School. The challenge of identifying the training needs of these heads of department in secondary schools remained my highest priority in these last two phases of the study.

## Statement Four

Staff management I'm worried about more than anything else ... this is so in a lot of schools ...

The management of people can be a bland and portmanteau-type phrase when used by professional people, and therefore a major reason for including this statement was to give heads of department the opportunity to elucidate precise areas of concern. Already the phrase 'handling people' has frequently been used when considering previous statements, and from this phrase has crystallized such activities and skills as staff appraisal, staff development, counselling and evaluation. It was hoped that statement four would be the means of throwing into sharp focus specific training needs of departmental heads which would not only reinforce what had aleady been noted but may also highlight other training needs not already considered to be of major importance.

The words 'I've had to learn to deal with colleagues because I'm dependent upon them' was a fundamental affirmation which every head of department would agree with who wished to develop a strong departmental team. This was the evidence established in this section of the study, yet many heads of department had declared in various ways that 'what worries me is that I may have to consult another teacher and say I am unhappy with what you are doing.'

Counselling staff was a skill desperately needed by most heads of department which formed an integral part of their desire to appraise their colleagues. In addition to the important skills of team building, the management skills of evaluation and delegation also come to the fore.

81

## An Ethnographic Study

## Statement Five

  Delegation ...something one has to be careful about ...

From the data collected in the previous three phases of the study, and in this present phase, it was apparent that the practice or non-practice of delegation affected many other management roles. It was not surprising, therefore, that this statement provoked the most discussion of all the seven statements on the "Comments Sheet". The intensity of discussion also reflected the concern expressed in previous phases about inter-personal skills and in particular the subject of delegation. The actual phrase, 'something one has to be careful about', suggests overtones of difficulties implicit in the process of delegation, but interviewees did not simply respond to the statement by focussing on areas of difficulty.

In their responses, department heads sought to justify their own particular practice or non-practice and shared their present experiences. A minority felt able to philosophize about the practice of delegation, and in so doing discussed the relationship of delegation to staff development and team building. However, an appreciation of delegation as an integral part of a process of staff appraisal was only tentatively referred to by one.

A prevailing attitude was noted in the words: 'I delegate those aspects of my job which I don't want responsibility for'. This suggested that there was a limited understanding of the purpose of delegation. Furthermore, to perceive the underlying message in the comment:

  There's a joke ... you only ask those (departmental
  members) who are likely to say 'yes' (to delegated
  tasks) ...

was that the constraint of professional autonomy was being registered. The inhibiting effect of this particular constraint was observed in other areas of managerial practices and will be considered in the next chapter. The use of excessive time in the process of delegation, hence the importance of time management, and the implication for team building - 'If he does not delegate, he will destroy the team' - were two other management tasks inextricably bound up with the process of delegation. All these recurring management practices were important, but in particular, the practice of delegation which warranted a detailed analysis amongst their major training needs.

## Statement Six

To be quite honest, I don't know what managing really means

This statement gave heads of department an opportunity not only to share their views on management, but also to display their attitudes towards their role as manager. Possible responses to this quotation could be to agree with the whole statement, agree in part or disagree totally, in which case I would encourage the interviewee to share his view and experience of managing a department. In fact there was another type of response which was initially to be neutral but thereafter to be critical of the school's organization and about the concept of management. This general statement following the specific statements about delegation, served its planned purpose, that is, drawing heads of department to share their problems, views and aspirations about management and themselves as managers.

Collating the various interviewees' responses, the first group of respondents agreed that they didn't understand what managing really meant. 'I didn't and I don't know whether I really do know what managing is ... in some ways I haven't been given a manager's job' was expressed by one who had been in post for eight years. Similar views were shared by about one third of the interviewees and gives weight to the vagueness of the head of department role as well as highlighting

the lack of confidence they had in their work. An even
clearer admission that management training was not understood
and had not been undertaken, came from another interviewee:
'I don't know what it (management) means; I work by instinct
and apply commonsense in managing people.'

In the group of interviewees who had taken a neutral stance
to statement six a typical response was that:

> My department is coping; getting on with the job ...
> but who evaluated what we have managed? We complain
> that we have no guidance ... we can always shelter in
> vagueness or behind someone ... guidelines of head of
> department's role would help ... it would be nice to
> know the expectations of managing.

This comment was not just an implied criticism of the senior
management team at Hodsom High School, but was made as a
general criticism about the evolving role of middle managers
in schools. A characteristic of those who took a neutral
stance was to pose rhetorical questions which showed uncertainty of what managing meant.

> Does it mean that one is making sure you've got the
> techniques to make people do what you want them to do?
> That is a crude but pure definition of managing, or is
> it more co-operation; the art of getting a microcosm
> of society, if you like, operating smoothly, so that
> everybody does not artificially feel that they are
> being jollyied along but actually feel that they are
> genuinely part of the whole and a responsible part of
> the whole? Sometimes people feel that they have been
> manipulated, manoeuvred and I do not think that this
> is good management.

For those who claimed to know the significance of 'managing',
their main thrust of interpretation focussed on the

management of people. Managing was described by an experienced head of department as being able to use 'techniques to make people do what you want them to do ... or is it causing co-operation? ... sometimes people think that they have been manipulated.'

Another head of department of a large department thought that

> Managing means ... I feel that I should be harder on people ... I'm too soft ... I'm not ruthless enough ... I want the job done; please do it. I question myself: the way I relate to members of my department and how they relate to me ... whether I'm using resources here to maximum efficiency.

These are the views of a hard working and conscientious interviewee who liked to lead his department from the front. This person wanted to go on management courses but he considered the demands in school too great to do so. Further quotations from interviewees who claimed that they knew the meaning of managing, highlighted a range of issues which others mentioned in their interviews.

> Management for me is being able to have a relationship with people; it is an awareness of the pressure on yourself and on other people ... to use the strengths of subordinates on behalf of children. Awareness of the deadlines where standards stand or fall ... it is being able to say, 'Well done!', when tasks are well done. Telling them (departmental members) when their responsibilities have not been fulfilled to your expectations.

The management skills of evaluation and staff appraisal are implied in this quotation but it was noted that there was a great discrepancy between the interviewee's aspirations and what actually happened in practice.

## An Ethnographic Study

Quotations in statement six gave some heads of department much food for thought and others concern about their present experience and responsibility for the professional development of colleagues. One in his second middle management post of his career said:

> Statement six worries me. Before you get to a middle
> manager you have to think the (expectations of the
> post) thing through ... It's about organising people
> so that they reach maximum potential if they can; so
> that they can gain success; that their opinions count;
> that they can organise themselves.

This reaction was an exception to the general responses and showed insight into the process of consulation and negotiation. However the theory of management practices by this individual did not match his practice.

> How do you interpret 'managing'? ... I've got some
> idea ... it depends on the person or individual ... if
> you make a mistake some people blame others ...
> perhaps one of the skills of management is to cover up
> (mistakes) ... some people will do anything to say
> they are not having problems ...

This quotation illustrated the confusion in the minds of heads of department when the concept of management was discussed. Management for most people was an uneasy term to accept and use. They so often saw themselves as master teachers rather than middle managers and lacked confidence in the role. Another fact of note was that departmental staff success in their work was rarely acknowledged by middle management, and failures were often quickly forgotten. This latter finding again highlighted the confusion in which many heads of department found themselves, lacking management skills and techniques and role identity.

In conclusion, statement six caused heads of department to share their fears, ignorance and aspirations. Managing people

# An Ethnographic Study

was emphasized as their greatest concern and I received specific requests that they should be given appropriate training to boost their confidence and expertise. This data underlined my view that there was a large gulf between what management skills heads of department thought was necessary in fulfilling their role, and their actual practice at Hodson High School.


## Statement Seven

You are not supposed to admit that you are not effective sometimes.

This final statement gave heads of department an opportunity to raise areas of their own weaknesses in an unthreatening way, and also to elaborate on any matters discussed in the previous statements. Implicit and explicit in their responses was the importance of their professional training, and the lack of it as experienced by those interviewed.

Hodson High School was a caring school, which cared for its students, and a senior management team who cared about the staff. However, a typical response from an interviewee was:

I think you ought to be able to (admit when you are not effective), but who could you go to, to get a sympathetic ear? I suppose my way of getting help is to moan in the staff room; have a grumble about something. I certainly feel better afterwards, but wheher this is an effective way is another matter.

Making individual problems and difficulties of public concern in the staff room had been noted from an early stage in phase one, and demonstrated the unstructured way in which difficulties were shared. However, these problems tended to be of little consequence, and referred to others' incompetence but not of the head of department. Weaknesses on their part were kept to themselves, and the surprise displayed by them that their peer group shared similar problems to themselves was most marked during this phase of the study.

The reasons given for not wishing to admit to ineffective practice centred around a feeling that they lacked confidence.

> I suppose there is a fear; it's a human nature thing. I admit to failure and can learn from it, but I never admit failure to members of my own department ...it's a matter of confidence and failure being equated with weakness.

Another interviewee explained:

> I'm confident when people are confident in me ... I would like to feel that there are occasions when I can say to a colleague this was a total flop ... but you have to have the confidence to do that.

Confidence can be the product of an individual's personality, but it can come about through staff appraisal and the recognition of a job well done. In addition, it was thought that confidence might be gained by having experienced professional training, thus creating competence in practising roles. The admission by most interviewees that they had not received professional training to become heads of department and that they desired such training could well support the logic that competence in professional managerial practice will create confidence in themselves.

A minority view was expressed by one who claimed to be competent and confident in his work: 'Who is it that you can keep your mistakes from ... I'm sorry about that one (statement seven).'

However, the feelings and thoughts of the majority was summed up by the view that:

# An Ethnographic Study

> Number seven (statement) stands out ... the stigma of
> the profession ... but if only heads (headteachers)
> would make a point of seeing heads of department once
> a term. It's true throughout the profession ... praise
> rare, criticism frequent. Perhaps that is the reason
> why you mistrust (people) ... lack confidence ...
> accept that you are not effective. People snapping at
> your heels ... people (H.o.D.'s) are afraid of
> consequences.

The desire for regular and constructive staff appraisal, not
only to create the possibility of praise and encouragement
but to establish an individual professional career development within the context of a caring and professional environment came across strongly. Through such a system strengths
and weaknesses could be acknowledged and training accepted as
an integral part of professional development.

Heads of department had identified themselves with the phase
one data used to compile the seven statements on a "Comments
Sheet". They were frank and honest with their responses and
three interviews exceeded the one hour allocated for each
interview. At the conclusion of this phase of the study
approximately half of the interviewees expressed a view that
'this paper (the "Comments Sheet") has made me think about my
role'. These reactions were made in the spirit of appreciation, having had to consider the roles they were practising;
why they were practising them, and how well they were
practising them. Such 'prompts' within their individual
professional careers had been absent.

It was again apparent to me that heads of department were
confused about their role definition, lacked confidence in
practising management skills, experienced role conflict and
desired guidance to solve their present experience of feeling
incompetent in their role. Stress was observed in their
feeling 'squeezed' as a middle manager and this experience
was made more acute by their preference to be master teachers

rather than middle managers.

I perceived that there was a large gulf between the management practices heads of department believed were necessary to
be effective in their role and what they were actually able
to practise. These shortcomings were acknowledged by interviewees and there was a resounding need recorded for regular
training of middle managers both prior to and after taking up
post. During the course of this phase of the study, no other
major training need came to the fore, and it was significant
that interviewees omitted to reflect upon the skill of
negotiation which in essence they desired in the management
of their departmental staff.

## Phase Five — Semi-structured Interviews with Members of the Senior Management Team

Members of the senior management team (S.M.T.) participated
in unstructured interviews of phase one when they were asked
two things:

1. Tell me what you do.

2. Tell me about your work with middle managers at Hodson
   High School.

I thought it of importance to interview the S.M.T. again to
probe further into their perspective of middle management
practices and their own involvement with heads of department.
The same process and method of semi-structured focussed
interviews used in phase four was used again here. Statements
made by members of the S.M.T. in phase one and representing a
common view of the group were collated and a short list of
three quotations was made from sixteen. These three quotations were chosen to give interviewees an opportunity to
develop their views on the role of middle managers at Hodson
High School, as well as to explain their perceived working

## An Ethnographic Study

relationships with them. In addition to these three quotations I designed two questions to give a further dimension to the chosen area of study, the training needs of heads of department.

## Statement One

Founder members (H.o.D.'s) have grown into their roles ...

In considering this statement, interviewees compared and contrasted the performance of all heads of department currently on the staff. They also made an assumption that heads of department had grown alongside or within the development of the school's organization, without an analysis of specific areas of growth or development. Although this 'taken-for-granted' view that professionals will cope with their roles, ironically they were critical about where and when heads of department failed to fulfil their roles.

Six key topics emerged during the course of discussion on this statement:

    accountability
    appraisal
    delegation
    evaluation
    job description
    teacher professional autonomy

It was clear that the S.M.T. found many difficulties and frustrations when working with middle management, in part, due to their own poor management, in part, to the assumption they made that master teachers were always effective middle managers, and an allied problem, an inability to identify effectively heads of department's training needs and promote appropriate training. It was suggesteded by the S.M.T. that job descriptions could be inhibiting instruments as opposed

to creative and positive motivators following a negotiated
expectation of role. However, interviewees thought that
middle management accountability to the S.M.T. was important,
and as one person said

> I want to pin people (H.o.D's) down to 'when' and
> 'why' ... we have a lot of good intentions with a lot
> of loose screws ... that's the trouble ... how to
> tighten up the screws without spoiling the ambiance of
> the organisation.

Both implicit and explicit reference was made to delegation;
it was implied that the work of departments had been totally
delegated to heads of department. However, feedbck was required from them. Conscious of maintaining high staff morale,
it was said that

> It is easy not to give enough praise (to H.o.D's and
> departmental members) ... but I don't find out about
> professional activities because heads of department
> don't tell me. I value it when a head of department
> says so-and-so is doing well. Sometimes they (H.o.D's)
> think I automatically know. I don't know how to remedy
> this ... we must think how best to communicate praise.

Such comments not only focus on delegation and accountability
but implicitly encompass staff appraisal and evaluation. The
need for heads of department to evaluate the work of their
departments was firmly believed by senior management to
assist in the process of head of department's professional
development, but they were never given cause to evaluate
their work. This became apparent when the term 'growth of
heads of department' was used on a number of occasions. For
example,

> We (S.M.T.) are feeling ... I am feeling that in the
> past two years I haven't thought carefully enough
> about the consequences of growth ... a cosy
> arrangement exists (referring to the environment and

organization at Hodson High School) ... one can't get
away with things which need to be sharpend up.

All members of the S.M.T. referred in various ways to founder
members who

... are now rather stale and jaded ... some
desperately looking for new openings ... a number of
heads of department are getting burnt out ... running
out of steam ... I don't know what the answer is to
keep them vibrant until some of them obtain other
posts.

A log jam in the promotion of teachers due to falling student
rolls  in secondary schools was a contributory factor in some
heads of department not gaining promotion, but  whatever  the
circumstances,  logistically  some  heads  of  department may
never gain further promotion. The rhetorical  question,  'How
does  one  maintain  vibrant  middle  management?',  remained
firmly with the S.M.T. of Hodson  High  School,  and  may  be
re-phrased  to  read,  'How  can heads of department gain job
satisfaction in their role?'

This situation highlighted a  shallow  understanding  of  the
head  of  department role, but, more importantly, the lack of
perception of their training needs. The notion that  'founder
members  have  grown  into  their  roles ...', proved to be a
vague feeling, and was  unsubstantiated  by  members  of  the
S.M.T. from a management perspective, because they had failed
to identify the training needs of heads of department.

## Statement Two

... keeping an eye on the training of probationary
teachers (heads of department's role) ... to keep an eye
on personnel ...

## An Ethnographic Study

This quotation was included for comment as Hodson High School had a large turn over of probationary teachers; 'We have wave upon wave of probationary teachers'; which gave heads of department frequent opportunity to be involved in the induction and appraisal of these teachers. It was hoped that the S.M.T. comments on this quotation would declare their expectations of heads of department in performing a middle management role such as appraiser, co-ordinator and staff developer. These specific roles would involve such managment skills as consultation, counselling, evaluation and negotiation.

The response of the S.M.T was to assume that heads of department were able to cope with management skills to enable them to induct probationary teachers into the profession, as well as caring for the other personnel in the department. Their expectations were that

> We require heads of department to keep 'a book' on them ... preparation before lessons and a post mortem afterwards ... We also need a day-to-day eye kept on them with informal advice on a daily basis. Heads of department have got to have time to sit down quietly with probationers ... a weekly review check ... how have you got on this week? ... retrospective and prospective. Two minutes in the loo is unacceptable.

Subsumed within such words as 'post mortem' and 'review' are again the skills of evaluation, counselling and appraisal, but these specific skills were not mentioned. Criticism too of heads of department was vague and lacked precision. There was no specific reference to an analysis of specific difficulties experienced by heads of department, and senior management were apparently unable to offer training facilities to rectify what for them was unsatisfactory middle management practices.

# An Ethnographic Study

## Statement Three

> ... must watch that we do not get stagnant ... the
> problem is keeping people's interest fresh ...

The latter phrase of the quotation complements the first
phrase and was chosen for its potential to act as a catalyst
to develop several strands of thought. These views could
range from staff training and professional development to the
management of change and delegation. The general reaction to
the quotation was to focus upon staff development. Many heads
of department had reached a plateau in their career, having
completed seven or eight years service at Hodson High School
with the possibility of promotion limited by falling student
rolls in secondary schools. These circumstances clearly
presented problems but also opportunities and challenges -
'preparing them for their next move', 'keeping people's
interest fresh' - but there were no specific suggestions made
about such preparation in terms of training or a correlation
between the skills and techniques required of their present
roles with that of possible future roles within the teaching
profession. Job rotation was considered by one interviewee,
but it was not thought to be an effective long-term solution
to the present problem under discussion.

The S.M.T. believed that INSET was essential for heads of department to remain vibrant. An assumption remained that heads
of department would perceive their own needs as professional
teachers and that new challenges related to the curriculum
would provide the stimulus to lead their departments. However, it would appear that the perceived problems of maintaining staff morale and efficient middle management would
remain until middle managers practised such skills as evaluation and delegation grew in confidence and gained greater
job satisfaction. Alternatively, S.M.T. would need to take an
active role in systematically identifying the training needs
and making provision for those needs.

95

# An Ethnographic Study

## Statement Four

What are the most important criteria used when
appointing a head of department?

The purpose of asking this question was to note whether the
management skills, which heads of department perceived to be
important but found difficult to implement, were also highlighted by the S.M.T. In part this question had already been
answered for, having had the opportunity earlier to monitor
the head of department appointments at Hodson High School, I
had obtained a list of criteria published for the guidance of
the Interviewing Panels. These criteria reflected the thinking of senior management about the experience and skills
needed of a head of department.

The first and most important criteria given by interviewees
was that heads of department should be good classroom
teachers. The second given by every one of them was that a
head of department should show leadership and have 'the
ability to communicate effectively on curricular innovations;
to have an easy rapport on a day-to-day basis with colleagues
...' Although specific skills were not mentioned the
importance of a department functioning as a team was strongly
emphasized. A third major group may be categorized as
inter-personal skills

> Heads of department need to keep an eye on personnel
> ... need to keep an eye on the ethos of belonging ...
> done not by formal meetings but general rapport
> created by constant caring ...

## Statement Five

What are the present training needs of heads of
department at Hodson High School?

# An Ethnographic Study

At the outset, in answering this question, interviewees gave general responses, for example, 'All staff have a need for training ... fulfilling their philosophy of the school ... a requirement for students and staff'. The level of reaction then moved to rhetorical statements, such as, 'INSET can increase the possibility of job satisfaction and in addition create job enlargement'. After much cautious approaches they became more specific with their comments. A key training need identified by the majority of the senior management was expressed by one in this way

> Good practice in the classroom is facilitated in the success of the teacher knowing what he is going to teach; who he is going to teach; how he is going to teach and how students best learn ...

CLearly the position of head of department as master teacher was of the greatest importance. It was noted that the skills of classroom management was a means by which heads of department may become staff developers, an important expectation among senior managers.

It became apparent that the next most important training need was awareness of the needs of departmental members.

> Heads of department need to latch onto ... to sharpen up ... to appreciate resource needs of people ... day-to-day issues ... briefing supply teachers, setting up probationers ... some heads ... live hand to mouth.

Such comments highlighted the need for acquisition of a range of managerial skills ranging from counselling and appraisal to delegation and evaluation. A head of department also had responsibility for the quality of education within his department as well as the welfare and professional development of collegues.

It became apparent from the data in earlier phases that heads

of department experienced difficulties in handling personal
staff relationships, a fact which was re-inforced in these
interviews with senior management.

> My meetings with heads of department often are crisis
> management problems ... problems with a teacher ...
> very often a personal relationship issue ...
> curriculum problems tend to be more gentle ...
> Personal problems are much sharper and immediate ...
> It seemed to me important that heads of department
> need to understand the implications and relationships
> of persons in the school structure.

To sum up, what came over strongly from these interviews was
that 'all was not well' with the general performance of heads
of department yet S.M.T. seemed unable to create a framework
to identify and meet their training needs. A caring
environment for individuals and a consultative management
style was both advocated and sought. Although their working
relationship with heads of department was good, evaluation of
standards of performance was gauged by a 'sixth sense' for
there was no planned structure, processes or defined method
by which to appraise their work.

The role of the head of department was perceived as that of a
master teacher rather than as a middle manager, consequently
clear expectations for them to be middle managers were not
apparent. It was assumed that a good teacher would make a
good manager and, therefore, the effective practice of innovation and delegation, for example, would just happen.
Although senior management perceived that heads of department
in fulfilling expressive roles were often uncomfortable and
lacking in confidence, they had not diagnosed specific
management problems nor were they able to detail training
needs to support them.

# 6 STRENGTHS AND WEAKNESSES IN THE MIDDLE MANAGEMENT ROLE

The assumptions, perceptions and attitudes of heads of department were gleaned from a range of sources, sometimes from
direct statement during interview sessions, but often by in-
direct implication. I gained much material from data collected from departmental members focussing on their experiences
of working in departments, and to a lesser extent from information which I had gathered from senior management
members. In addition, during the course of their work, I was
able to tease out feelings and views held by departmental
heads. It is of particular note that often the assumptions
made by heads of department were the root cause of their
difficulties, and also highlighted the conflict between their
'desire' for good management practice on the one hand and
what in fact was reality on the other. This study effectvely
penetrated the everyday 'taken-for-granted' aspects of the
work of heads of department.

## Preparation for the Role of Head of Department

From the empirical study on Hodson High School the most
significant finding is that heads of department were unprepared and indeed felt unprepared for their role. Even
after a period of eight years in post, they were saying that
they had neither learnt about nor been initiated into

significant aspects of their work. The school governors and senior management team in making head of department appointments gave scant consideration to short-listed candidates as middle managers, the emphasis being on that of master teacher. This suggested that they assumed that good Master Teachers made good Middle Managers. Training for the role of head of department was assumed not only by the school governors and senior management, but also by the L.E.A. The latter did not make provision for training, and in the words of one interviewee: 'This shows you just how important the Authority rates our job.'

The establishment of an induction course for all new heads of department appointed to Hodson High School was specifically suggested by heads of department on three separate occasions during interview sessions. All with at least six years in post, their suggestion came as a result of a declared unease about 'handling people'. A further suggestion that an induction of heads of department should be carried out by their peer group pre-supposed that they had the necessary skills to do this work. However, notwithstanding poor management skills, what was, in fact, being suggested for an induction course was a 'survival kit', sharing the institutional expectations, routines and traditions, and not the skills of management practices. Their instrumental role was considered by most heads of department to be more important than their expressive role, because the routine day-to-day administrative work, if ignored, would be quickly observed by other staff. They believed too that they were effective in instrumental roles, which makes a natural reason for omitting management skills related to their expressive role.

Preparation in the skills of management for the role of head of department prior to appointment was not an accepted practice, nor was it acknowledged to be necessary by appointing bodies, since they assumed that potential heads of department had already acquired these skills. The senior management team at Hodson High School did not provide an induction course nor an on-going staff development programme

## Strengths and Weaknesses

for heads of department who were their middle managers.
Ironically, it was upon these middle managers that they
depended to implement school policy. Both heads of department
and departmental members agreed that training was required
for them to be effective middle managers, although they did
not use the specific term 'training'. It was clear therefore
that it could not be taken for granted that a master teacher
would be an effective middle manager, and that heads of
department required management skills and techniques to be
effective, especially in their expressive roles.

## Schools as Organizations

Heads of department showed little awareness that their 'taken
for granted' assumptions about organizations were coloured by
inherited past practice and custom. There was also little
evidence of an awareness that there were differing paradigms
of how organizations work. It was evident that no in-service
work had been received which would create such awareness. For
example, that a system structuralist approach to organizations practised by the great majority of heads of department
was not the only way to perceive the working of an organization.

In the staff handbook at Hodson High School there was a
simple, clear and uncluttered organizational chart of the
school's hierarchical structure. The headteacher explained
that the chart was

> The normal thing to help new staff to understand the
> lines of communicaton in the school and to give the
> newcomer, particularly the probationary teacher, a
> sense of coherence of the school's organization.

For the heads of department the organizational chart displayed power bases, with the head having the greatest power.
Heads of department assumed comparative power within their
designated domains, and their role culture (see Handy, 1984)

## Strengths and Weaknesses

re-inforced the stratification of power bases assumed by them. It did not suggest the development of a coherent organization desired by the senior management team; on the contrary, it fragmented the organization, since they did not perceive their 'power bases' as being integral to the whole school organization. Individual power bases were considered by most heads of department to be crucial in the process of maintaining departmental boundaries, but this in turn re-inforced isolation between departments and the feeling of being threatened by other departments. Assumptions made from a narrow departmental perspective limited both individual and group potential in developing many aspects of their work.

Failure to transmit and interpret school policy to departmental members caused obstruction to senior management plans, while the inability of heads of department to exercise effectively managerial skills within departments further threatened the implementation of school policy. Indeed the power of the school's hierarchy was very much dependent upon the effective performance of its middle managers, a fact realized by the senior management but not fully grasped by departmental heads as they projected an insular departmental perspective.

Implicit in what has been recorded about their positon of power within a hierarchy was that heads of department frequently assumed that they operated in a vacuum. They believed they had power and authority, but this was in fact eroded through their deficient management skills. Another assumption was their understanding of the school organization as a static concept and roles within it having a fixed status. A flexible organizational structure of secondary schools, as for example suggested by Dennison (1985), was alien to the thinking amongst most of them. A perception of a fixed status of roles also came through in conversation about career prospects. They also projected the perspective of a functionalist, seeing people's behaviour shaped by the departmental system of the school's organization. Ironically, heads of department claimed to desire to interact with

## Strengths and Weaknesses

members of their own deparment and with other departments. However, the practice of negotiation, for example, was rarely observed even though many meetings occurred in the daily round of the school's routine.

That 'Cultural confusion is one of the principal ills that plague organisations' (Handy, 1984) was a true reflection of life at Hodson High School. This was manifest in the criticism of senior management by heads of department over consultation and by departmental staff about heads of department. It was apparent that there was a genuine desire by senior management for a consultative style of management to operate within the school organization, but heads of department did not appreciate the value of interaction within the process of consultation. It was probably less than a coincidence, therefore, that heads of department felt confident in the instrumental tasks such as examination entries and caring for stock, but uneasy with their expressive roles such as delegation and team building where interaction with individuals was required.

Another significant assumption which heads of department made about their departmental organization was that they considered themselves to be in 'primus inter pares relationship' with the senior management team at the expense of the pastoral year heads. The year heads received the same Grade IV Burnham responsibility allowance as the majority of departmental heads, and on the school organizational chart they were on a par with each other; heads of department accountable to the Deputy Head (Curriculum), the year heads accountable to the Deputy Head (Pastoral). Friction between heads of department and year heads over students' disipline in the classroom was noted on a number of occasions . Heads of year claimed that this was the responsibility of the head of department, whilst the majority of heads of department considered that their job was to get on with the job of teaching and not to be thwarted by student behavioural problems. Another example where the status of these two middle management roles came into sharp focus and conflict was over the fourth year option choices.

## Strengths and Weaknesses

Questions arose over who had the greatest authority, the head of department who had made professional predictions about students' future educational career, albeit from the narrow perspective of their specialized subject, or the year head whose task was to ensure that students had a balanced curriculum. The head of department had an academic authority, the year head a personal authority. The strength of the individual personality, not rational argument or negotiation, generally decided these issues, and again heads of department displayed their insular perception of the school's organization.

In referring to pastoral roles, H.M.I. records: 'This extension of "middle management" roles has to some extent reduced the status and influence of heads of department.' (Welsh Office, 1984) This view coincided with the assumptions of heads of department at Hodson High School; and a further reason for a perceived erosion of their status was the departmental membership of year heads and members of the senior management team. The presence of senior colleagues and members of their peer group within a departmental team, albeit part-time members, created much unease for them. They assumed a fixed perspective of formal roles and felt unable to co-ordinate the departmental work of their senior colleagues or peer group. Ironically, senior colleagues and members of their peer group declared that they would have welcomed guidance and constructive support from their head of department. The inability to co-ordinate departmental work was partly due to their lack of managerial skills, in part a lack of confidence to carry out such work, but also due to their limited perspective of organizational paradigms.

A final observation was that heads of department assumed the school organization to reflect a line management model rather than a collegiate model (see Harries-Jenkins, 1970). A considerable emphasis on hierarchy has been noted, and the assumed increased power and rewards which were obtained on entry to the higher positions within the hierarchy. 'Reports sent up and instructions sent down' was considered to be the

## Strengths and Weaknesses

method of operation. A strong expectation that senior management should carry out punitive measures on those members of staff who failed in their roles was expressed by many heads of department. What was not observed during the course of the study was a comparative sense of responsibility based on individual professional standards: the hallmark of the collegiate model.

To sum up the great majority of heads of department assumed school organizations to be simple hierarchies with fixed roles. Their departments were seen as insular units within the organization, and accountabilities and relationships across the organization were not thought to be of signi-ficance. The environment and people as individuals were frequently thought to be separate and apart from the concept of organization. All these factors contributed towards a limited perspective which heads of department had acquired about their role, and in consequence led to their insecurity as middle managers. Another consequence was minimal job satisfaction and frustration.

## Relationships with People

Eight years on from the inauguration of Hodson High School, a full complement of eighty six staff had been appointed and a bureaucratic role culture had replaced the initial corporate social-type relationships amongst staff. The staffroom and the school environment was still friendly and relaxed but below the surface were significant undercurrents of tension. The majority of heads had been there since the inauguration and hence with eight years experience behind them; the euphoria had faded; the experience of feeling 'burnt out' yet desiring promotion created a dilemma in that they felt it incumbent upon themselves to maintain a facade of 'energetic aspiration'. The 'organizational underworld', the world of micropolitics (see Hoyle, 1986) inhabited by heads of department was complex and displayed the relationships they had with members of their role set and their peers.

## Strengths and Weaknesses

### Relationships between heads of department

Most heads of department, as we have seen, defended their own departmental boundaries. This insular attitude resulted in a basic fear that members of their peer group were seeking to out-manoeuvre them, contending for limited resources which included finance, accommodation and staffing. In interview sessions it was divulged which members of staff habitually made appointments to see the headteacher; and frequently, seemingly light-hearted exchanges observed between colleagues were an attempt to find out why a colleague had seen the headteacher. Despite the continual round of consultative meetings they feared they knew little of the school's development. This fear and mistrust affected relationships between members of the peer group and with members of the senior management team. The effect of some seeking promotion within the school and elsewhere contributed to the complexity of the micropolitics of the school organization.

A most significant assumption heads of department made about one another was that their colleagues experienced minimal problems in performing their roles. In fact this proved to be a false assumption, as every head of department, bar one, shared their unease in fulfilling expressive roles. Concealing failure and difficulties in performing management practices from one another was an attempt in part to maintain a professional pride under the cloak of professional autonomy, ·partly because they believed that an admission of failure would jeopardize potential chances of promotion, but also in part due to the absence of a school staff development plan and the availability of management training courses.

### Relationships with senior management

There was a distinct message of 'them' and 'us' when one looked at this relationship. The perceived role strata of the bureaucratic school organization helped to create this gulf. Most heads of department were unable to think and react

## Strengths and Weaknesses

positively to whole-school issues, for their perspectives were limited to within their own departmental boundaries. On occasions mistrust and aggression occurred because they were unable to stretch out to gain a deeper perspective of the school's work, thus affecting their relationships with senior colleagues. A classic example was the method of distributing the school's capitation. Inevitably there will be differing viewpoints on issues between individuals within an organization, but the predominant thrust of comments from heads of department was that senior management did not sufficiently understand their role. On reflection, this gulf between middle and senior management was inevitable as senior management themselves had been heads of department and had themselves suffered from lack of role definition.

Heads of department having created an isolationist position for themselves yet believed that they had a good understanding of the role of senior management and of their subordinates, but not so clear what their own role should be. Senior management were expected to take punitive measures when mistakes were made within the organization and criticism was levelled against them for not fulfilling this expectation. Ironically, heads of department often wished to opt out of their own responsibility of controlling staff, seeking to maintain a low profile. Too often a scapegoat was sought in senior management which did not enhance good working relationships with the latter, nor develop the skills of problem solving as a corporate activity, thus creating the opportunity to bridge the gap between the 'them' and 'us'.

## Relationships with department members

Relationships between heads of department and departmental members may be described as 'socially cordial'. Heads of department wished to be accepted and liked by their colleagues, and it is significant that the majority of them rarely used their head of department office, preferring to do their departmental business in the staff room. They were apparently

107

## Strengths and Weaknesses

always accessible to departmental staff, but the depth of conversations with them was shallow and generally consisted of routine matters. This situation reflects a formal/informal dichotomy where heads of department displayed unease in acting out a formal role and preferred to function in an informal way in a public place. In the open forum of the staff room 'We'll discuss that later' was frequently heard, but departmental members maintained that 'later' never occurred. Added to this scenario were the occasions when departmental problems, involving 'known' individuals, were aired in the staff room, all of which created tension and conflict between heads and their colleagues. Heads of department had already acknowledged that 'the most difficult part of the job of being a head of department is dealing with people'. They also admitted that they lacked trust in departmental members and this was particularly apparent over the restricted extent of delegation. Lack of trust in colleagues led to a restricted flow of communication, which in turn limited an understanding of people amd their current needs. Paradoxically, heads of department considered that departmental colleagues should be professional in their work.

Heads of department often wished to opt out of the overt responsibility of controlling staff, seeking to maintain a low profile. By withdrawing delegated tasks when their colleagues performed ineffectively they were in reality again distancing themselves from their colleagues. A junior colleague writing a scheme of work had the task withdrawn when it did not reach the expectations of the departmental head. Another example was a low level administrative task of examination entries which was similarly withdrawn in another set of circumstances, resultng in human relationships being damaged. In contrast was the aggressive power coersive approach of two heads of department where colleagues were told in no uncertain terms 'to get your act together'; but how the 'act' should be planned and implemented was not explained.

An assumption made throughout the role set - head of department, senior management, departmental member - was that

## Strengths and Weaknesses

people were rational and acted accordingly. This false assumption inevitably affected relationships between members of staff and often created a barrier to heads of department showing empathy towards colleagues. I also found that heads of department were prepared rarely to consider issues beyond their own personal departmental experiences in the process of justifying their 'professional' preferences in decision-making.

The functionalist approach of most assumed that a consensus view about organizations and people prevailed amongst colleagues, and their system's perspective of the school as departmental-based organization led them to understand their role as a formal position of authority within the hierarchy. Relationships between staff therefore were intrinsically relationships of power and the political dimension of inter-action was rarely addressed. I was frequently made aware of an autocratic approach towards departmental members. Heads of department remained trapped, 'Squeezed between departmental members and the hierarchy (senior management)', thus creating an uneasy relationship between members of the head of department role set. The unease experienced in dealing with colleagues was compounded through their lack of management skills which caused them to lack confidence and to feel uncomfortable in their relationships with colleagues.

## The Professional Autonomy of Teachers

Four specific issues came to the fore on numerous occasions during the course of the study which related to the autonomy heads of department believe they have as members of the teaching profession. This claim to professional autonomy extended to other teachers and affected the role of the head of department. Each of these issues are discussed below:

i) Reluctance to admit failure

This was one of the most significant findings to come out of

109

## Strengths and Weaknesses

the interviews. In other words, professionalism was a 'cloak of security' for many heads of department which frequently isolated them from their peers, subordinates and superiors. They believed that an admission of failure to one's superior could well jeopardize future promotion. Sharing uncertainties, or an error of judgement with subordinates, or superordinates might cause a lack of confidence in their leadership. 'I would be happy to talk with my wife that I had failed, but not to those you are responsible for or responsible to' was how one head of department expressed his feelings.

With this built-in fear of failing and admission of failure, they were seeking to maintain their autonomy. In doing so they were limiting their professional development since they were not acknowledging their weaknesses and were not themselves in a position where they might find help and support to improve their management skills, such as team building, delegation and negotiation. Often departmental members seemed very much aware of their departmental head's weaknesses. Moreover, it was significant that though heads of department claimed they would welcome guidance on their professional careers, they themselves had created a barrier preventing such guidance in their fear of admitting 'failure'.

The messages about the fear of failure given out by heads of department were so strong that a quotation 'You are not supposed to admit that you are ineffective sometimes ... ' was used in phase four interviews to give them an opportunity to develop their views on this subject. A typical response to the quotation was

> It (the comment) stands out ... the stigma of the
> profession ... you are always encouraged to share
> things if they go wrong, but then there's the problem
> which will go against you. If you (H.o.D.) tell
> somebody else and it gets escalated ... if you make a
> mistake you keep it to yourself and camouflage it ...
> what does that tell us about heads of department ...

## Strengths and Weaknesses

> Heads of department fail to realize the importance of
> middle management.

This personal view encapsulated the fears, frustrations and
yet awareness of departmental heads' potential as middle
managers.

### ii) The desire to preserve privacy

It was found that heads of department often displayed acute
embarrassment at having to appraise the work of probationary
teachers, a statutory obligation for the latter to experience
as well as a professional responsibility for heads of department if they accept the role of staff developer. Many claimed
that they could evaluate the work of colleagues without
entering a classroom; others made excuses to gain entry into
rooms claiming to need equipment from a stock cupboard.
Taking this attitude in a school which encouraged consultation and an open system of management highlighted the
strength of reticence of heads of department to perform the
roles of evaluator, staff developer and appraiser.

This reticence also concealed a degree of ignorance on how
the process of appraising staff might operate. During the
course of this study, the L.E.A. published a specimen report
based on the D.E.S. publication "The New Teacher in School"
(1982) for appraising probationary teachers' performance. The
senior management team at Hodson High School, conscious of
the problem of head of department involvement in the induction of probationary teachers, caused a senior teacher to
co-ordinate this work in the hope that things would improve.
However, the senior management did not plan any training to
support heads of department in the skills of appraising
staff.

Another area of concern was

> How to manage colleagues who do not hand work in on

> time ... those who do not mark their books regularly
> ... integrating those people with conflicting
> interests ... how do you get near them?

It was thought by many heads of department that techniques
for dealing with such problems would be most useful. From
behind the cloak of professionalism some, assuming that
departmental members had a competence to cope effectively in
the classroom, therefore took the attitude that there was no
need to be involved with the professional activities of
colleagues. Others knew that their colleagues were incompetent in aspects of their work but lacked the courage,
conviction and skills to rectify and improve those areas of
weakness.

iii) The option of practising INSET

Another way in which professional autonomy manifested itself
was in relation to in-service training. Heads of department
selected courses according to their perceived needs or
interest in their specialized subject. 'Management' was seen
as an all-embracing term which would supply the appropriate
knowledge for advancement in the profession. This attitude of
teachers was also found in the work of Hilsum and Start
(1974) and Dennison (1981), but it was interesting to note
that the emphasis was on 'knowing' rather than on 'doing'.
The professional autonomy of colleagues was a major barrier
which prevented heads of department from actually 'doing'
management practices, and the fear of admitting incompetence
was a barrier to the rather hollow plea that 'INSET has to
happen when there's a need'.

On numerous occasions after interview sessions with
departmental heads I was asked for career guidance. The
message came through clearly that they would have welcomed
career guidance and professional development much earlier in
their careers. The unstructured interview, they claimed,
caused them to think for the first time about the signifi-

112

## Strengths and Weaknesses

cance of their role and how well they were performing.
Departmental members also sought professional advice, which
suggested that members of the teaching profession welcomed
the opportunity to receive advice about their professional
development, but hitherto had accepted the belief that
serving time in the profession without training ensured
eventual promotion and effective practice.


 iv) The desire to preserve the staus quo

The fourth way in which professional autonomy was displayed
was through the role culture of the school's hierarchy. In
senior staff meetings, a forum in which heads of department
discussed organizational and curriculum issues, it was
observed that each head of department was 'fighting his own
corner'. For example, in the process of distributing
capitation allowances for the ensuing academic year, the aim
of a head of departmemt ranged from self preservation to
increased autonomy through financial departmental gain.

The infiltration of professional autonomy was further
observed in negotiations by senior management to innovate
integrated curricular courses. Curriculum development was
often obstructed by attempts to preserve their status quo.
Indeed, the role culture of departments nurtured professional
autonomy and restricted change and development. This led me
to ask the question 'Is the role of head of department
out-dated?' From the empirical evidence gathered in the
study, the answer would appear to be 'yes'; but the
implications of this answer would require a change in school
cultures to match the implementation of an alternative
team-leader concept.

Teacher professional autonomy would appear to be a deep
seated influence creating isolationalism amongst heads of
department, affecting their professional development and
their effectiveness as middle managers.

# 7 A LEADERSHIP ROLE

From the findings on, and conclusions of, the implications of
teacher professional autonomy, it was apparent that heads of
department had not thought through the consequences of this
practice, particularly its effects on the practice of leadership. The desires of all departmental heads at Hodson High
School were to be good leaders of their departments, but they
displayed little knowledge of techniques of leadership and
many seemed unaware of the effects of their present practice.
Indeed the concept of leadership was understood by most of
them in simplistic terms and the possibility of leadership
being a dynamic concept was a view not shared by the majority
of these middle managers. This view was also echoed by a
member of the senior management team

> Heads of department have got to be supportive ...
> they've got to know at what point they are in charge
> of the department and at what point they are part of
> the whole.

The question remained of when and how would heads of department come to this realization.

## A Dictator Role

The findings of this study supported the work of Howson
(1980) in that most heads of department assumed the role of

## A Leadership Role

'dictator' rather than 'democrat' (see also Howson and Woolnough, 1982). The majority of them perceived the concept of leadership at the front of the phalanx, and the possibility of being in the centre or rear of the column was not in keeping with their mode of leadership. 'Managers must manage and be seen to manage' was a phrase used by interviewees, highlighting this philosophy of leadership.

A hard working and conscientious head of department who liked to lead the department from the front thought that

> Managing means ... I feel that I should be harder on people ... I'm too soft ... I'm not ruthless enough ... I want that job done, please do it. I question myself: the way I relate to members of my department and how they relate to me ... whether I'm using resources here to maximum efficiency.

Another approach on leadership was recorded as 'I get satisfaction when I can manipulate my staff to do what I want ... but the main task is to motivate people ... ' Yet another view was 'I try to shame them into doing things ... of course, it could go the wrong way'. It was also noted that departmental heads' attitude towards consultation was reflected in their perceived stance on leadership:

> Consultation is a matter of how you carry out the solution of communicating decisions already made.

This approach, not surprisingly, provoked resentment amongst departmental members. 'He may be able to handle kids, but he's not always right when he's dealing with adults ...' was a reaction to the 'dictator-type' role assumed by most of the heads of department for most of the time.

## A Lack of Understanding

One basic reason for heads of department implementing a

## A Leadership Role

facile interpretation of leadership was their lack of knowledge of the plethora of literature on the subject of leadership. Fundamental routine tasks associated with a leadership
role often had not been accomplished. Departmental aims and
objectives had not been thought out, recorded, nor negotiated
with departmental members. A vague notion that 'We all (in a
department) need to be responsible as professionals', was a
glib desire for a coherent team practice but this attitude
fudged the issues of leadership towards agreed goals in an
environment where the professional autonomy of teachers
amongst departmental members was considered a right as a
result of initial professional teacher training. Some heads
of department acted on impulse, claiming to have little time
in which to think. However, it became clear that the
commitment of departmental heads was 'weighted' towards their
preferred activity of teaching rather than managing the work
of their departments in the process of leading members of
their departments.

## An Acceptance of Failure

In the confidence of interview sessions, a large number
shared their concern that they were falling short in their
leadership role. A lack of realistic planning led a large
number of them to experience 'burn out'. To say 'no' was
often interpreted by heads of department as a sign of
weakness on their part; it resulted in initiatives not being
sustained and created stress on them. This in turn raised
frustration on the part of both heads of department and
departmental members. Heads of department realized that
positive leadership was required from them but there was an
unease that the techniques and skills necessary to achieve
such qualities of leadership had not been acquired. Implicit
in what has been recorded was the fact that they lacked the
skill of prioritizing, as well as the ability to manage
people.

It could be argued that a reason why they were unsure about

## A Leadership Role

their leadership role was because their role was evolving, and a clear understanding of it could not be perceived. This may be true in part, but the attitudes of and the assumptions made by heads of department about organizations and people underpinned their limited perceptions about leadership. Another integral factor in identifying areas of weak leadership was the built-in role conflict of being both master teacher and middle manager; and it must be admitted that the majority declared a preference to be master teacher rather than middle manager. They did not take enough time to consider the implications of leadership, the way it should be practised by recognizing strengths and weaknesses of departmental members and by monitoring progress of their departments. It was too easy to lay blame on incompetent and unenthusiastic departmental members or just simply to say 'I do not have time to do my job'. The fact remains that the role of head of department requires a leadership role and that the quality of leadership reflects the quality of the department.

## A Leading Professional

If a distinction between the roles of leading professional and an administrator is acceptable (see Hughes in Bush, 1980 and Handy, 1984), then heads of department were indicating that they themselves were not developing nor being developed as leading professionals. With just two exceptions they all declared that they did not have the expertise of managing people in order to develop their colleagues within their departments. These circumstances were partly due to the absence of a staff development policy which was expressed in career terms: there was also an absence of any systematic form of staff appraisal in the school.

An attitude prevailed amongst departmental heads that staff development of colleagues was not part of their work, even though they clearly perceived that 'There's insufficient motivation for people on lower salary scales'.

117

# A Leadership Role

Who should cause staff development to happen in the school?
What should be the content of a staff development programme?
Whose needs should be met? The reaction of heads of department to these rhetorical questions was that this was the
responsibility of senior management. Much criticism was made
of heads of department by probationary teachers for not
exercising what they considered to be the duty of a leading
professional. They expected to receive guidance, support, and
a clear role expectation. Specific criticism was made about
those heads of department who failed to observe them teach,
as well as those who gained a superficial insight into their
classroom management. Many probationary teachers, and more
experienced teachers reflecting on their own probationary
period of service, thought that their head of department had
let them down as their leading professional.

It was interesting to note the expectations of teachers in
their second and ensuing years of teaching who wanted heads
of department to act as examplars and to be involved in
supporting them in their work. Members of the senior
management team and other experienced members of staff who
had a teaching commitment also expected the head of department to give them their professional advice.

> It is so often assumed that you keep abreast with your
> subject ... and although you may have taught for a
> long time you can become out of touch with current
> thinking ...

was the reaction of a pastoral head. Another thrust of
expectation was that opportunities of being involved in the
work of the department ought to be provided, hence offering
staff development. It was felt too that colleagues should be
given insight into the wider perspectives of the school. The
majority of heads of department restricted themselves to
working and thinking within their own departmental
boundaries, and thus were 'restricted' leading professionals,
unable to respond to their colleagues' expectations.

118

## A Leadership Role

The response of heads of department to these expectations of departmental members was predictable, that is in the sense that departmental members who had completed their probationary period of service would not expect heads of department to involve themselves in staff development, for it was tradition that professional autonomy maintained teacher privacy. A comment from a teacher in his second year of teaching that '(Lesson) Notes won't be looked at nor pupil exercise books', emphasized the embedded belief of the majority of teachers that heads of department would not involve themselves with staff development.

It was significant that there was a consensus view that many heads of department would welcome a policy of staff development whereby senior colleagues would acknowledge what individuals were actually achieving and where they were failing to perform effectively. In the latter circumstances, a number of interviewees suggested that senior staff were too kind to middle managers and were prepared to allow them to 'muddle along'. However, when a member of the senior management team implemented a 'let's get tough' staff development approach, heads of department withdrew within their professional autonomy cocoons.

## Curriculum Leader

There was little evidence from Hodson High School to show that heads of department were curriculum leaders. They were 'restricted' in much common debate with fellow heads of department in terms of an all-school curriculum. To engage in all-school curriculum activities was considered by some departmental members, and their views had been communicated to their respective heads of department, that this was a sign of weakness on their part. Defending departmental boundaries in order to secure financial resources, accommodation and staffing levels was a high priority engendered by the role culture of the school's hierarchy. This insular stance was a major factor in restricting the role of a curriculum leader

# A Leadership Role

for the majority of heads of department.

There did seem to be much staff discussion and consultation at this school, members of staff frequently complaining about the excessive number of meetings, and in their view, the inordinate amount of time used. The majority of departmental heads enjoyed a 'good discussion' on curriculum issues but there did appear to be a lack of ability on the part of the senior management to prioritize curriculum development and assist heads of department in following through agreed school curriculum policy.

The school had responded to the D.E.S. publication "The School Curriculum" (D.E.S.,1981) recording the school's curriculum aims and objectives, and there was much enthusiasm for curriculum development. This enthusiasm was reflected in the numerous departmental innovations, but the frequency and rapidity with which these innovations occurred limited the inability of heads of department's curriculum leadership. Such practice reflected a veneer of consultation and under-standing about the theory and practice of innovation. The confusion and frustration expressed by departmental members about curriculum development gave further evidence that heads of department were not fulfilling their curriculum roles.

The absence of explicit departmental aims and objectives led to further confusion amongst departmental members and heads of department themselves as many a department's work drifted from one situation to another without reflectng a clear departmental policy. Departmental members were 'au fait' with syllabuses which were to be followed, but, apart from two departments, effective schemes of work were not prepared. There was evidence that these circumstances resulted from ignorance of the difference between a syllabus and a scheme of work, but was also a result of weakness in developing team work, and in the chairing of departmental meetings. It was noted that heads of department took a sparse amount of time to plan and to pool ideas in order to improve both the quality of the curriculum and to establish an esprit de corps amongst departmental colleagues. In departmental discussions there was often a verbal acknowledgement of students' varying abilities and aptitudes, but this was not translated into a differentiated scheme of work to meet the range of student needs. This omission apparently was not a local issue but was ' a widespread and very serious problem' (D.E.S., 1985b).

Teacher professional autonomy was again very much in evidence when heads of department sought to develop a uniform approach to the assessment of students' work. Such phrases as 'I know my standards' and 'I am a hard marker', projected an auto-cratic attitude based on teacher autonomy. Not only was the problem of standardizing student assessment compounded by teacher autonomy, but this problem eminated from the absence of work with clear objectives. In part, heads of department lacked negotiating skills, and in part departmental members lacked assessment techniques. The limited amount of curri-culum evaluation practised resulted from a lack of leadership skills, a knowledge of the techniques of evaluation and an apparent inherent professional stigma impeding the develop-ment of the quality of the school curriculum. Again, this situation is not limited to a local scene, but would appear to be a national problem (D.E.S., 1982; Welsh Office, 1984; D.E.S., 1983a).

Departmental members in the study revealed that part-time members of staff and full-time colleagues working outside their specialisms were not supported by heads of department over curriculum matters. Requests for curriculum guidance were made by senior members of staff and departmental heads' peer group, but such colleagues inhibited the heads of department who assumed that their seniority in the school's hierarchy also gave them the authority and curriculum ex-pertise to deal adequately with their own deployed allocation of departmental work. The telling comment of one full-time member of staff working outside his specialist subject that 'with no support from my head of department I just avoid parts of the syllabus I'm not sure about ...' highlighted the importance of this particular problem.

## A Leadership Role

As the main thrust of the study was focussing on the expressive role of heads of department, instrumental roles have been omitted from this review, although it is acknowledged that there is no rigid demarcation between expressive and instrumental roles.

The assumption that the head of department, a master teacher, would be an effective curriculum leader was a false assumption. The accumulative effect of the problems experienced by heads of department recorded in this section contributed to their failure to exercise an effective curriculum leadership role. In addition, the inherent professional barriers of a predominant role culture in the school and the professional autonomy of colleagues also inhibited them in their curriculum leadership.

The great majority of heads of department viewed their present middle management role as a means of gaining promotion, and interpreted the concept of leading professional in a limited manner, as being equivalent to that of master teacher. Although they felt confident as master teachers, they did not use this position of strength as a leading professional. They were often frustrated and lacked confidence in performing their role as head of department, and it was thought - as if by magic - that the role of deputy head or senior teacher would present less tension than their currently perceived Janus-type role of having to meet the demands of both senior management and departmental staff. There was slight awareness that the next hierarchical position would also be a Janus-type role, presenting different demands, similar managerial skills, but also requiring the role of leading professional. There was also little percepton that their present work gave much opportunity to provide staff development for others, and in so doing cause staff development for themselves and an active role of leading professional.

# A Leadership Role

## Master Teacher - Middle Manager Role Conflict

As discussed earlier the role of head of department was an evolving one which caused role conflict, with individuals within a school's organization perceiving the role of head of department from various perspectives. The research studies of Lambert (1972), Siddle (1977), Howson (1980) and Archer (1981), to name but four, confirmed that role ambiguity was much in evidence and also caused role conflict. Headteachers and L.E.A. Advisory Officers' expectations were in conflict with those of heads of department. Added to these dimensions of role conflict was the built-in role conflict of master teacher and middle managers. Such was the background in which heads of department at Hodson High School had to act out their roles, whether they fully perceived these circumstances or not. However, they all did perceive some aspects of this role conflict, particularly in being a master teacher for at least eighty per cent of their school week, the remaining time being available for middle management responsibilities.

It has already been recorded that they desired an induction course for their peers, feeling under pressure themselves and realizing that they were not coping with the day-to-day work of the department. Members of the senior management team and officers of the L.E.A. had assumed that being a master teacher, the perceived basis upon which heads of department were appointed, was sufficient qualification to manage a department. Subsumed within this assumption was a further assumption that heads of department did not need training for their middle management role. Another strand in this morass of confusion, conflict and assumption was the practice of professional autonomy which prevailed amongst teachers at Hodson High School. Within the concept of teacher professional autonomy there were perceived ideas by some department heads that training was not required for effectively acting out their middle management role. Equally important to record was the assumption by many of them that once a teacher had been trained in a College or Department of Education there was no need for further training or intrusion into their

# A Leadership Role

classrooms, apart from assistance with disciplinary problems
with students. It was also assumed by some that the inauguration of a subject department automaticaly constituted a team
with very little management practice on their part.

These attitudes and beliefs held by heads of department
inhibited managerial roles such as evaluator, appraiser and
staff developer being developed and practised. For example,
when required to be an appraiser many were unable to fulfil
the role. Opinions formed about colleagues' capabilities were
made by uninformed judgements, such as heads of department
who attempted to appraise probationary teachers without ever
having watched them teach. Lack of trust in their departmental members was perceived to be a major factor inhibiting the
practice of delegation. There was, also, not surprisingly, an
apparent lack of trust by departmental members in their
departmental heads who, they believed, often were not equal
to their tasks as middle managers. Such was the often
frustrating and uncertain circumstances in which members of
the role set - senior management, head of department and
departmental members found themselves; thus exacerbating the
master teacher, middle manager role conflict.

Conclusions drawn from the above record show the middle
management role of heads of department as the subordinate,
'undernourished' without training, occasionally not recognized as existing due to lack of time, acquired knowledge and
skills. Heads of department declared that they enjoyed their
teaching; they felt confident in the classroom: 'This is the
job for which I have been trained'. In contrast, frustration
was observed 'when administrative tasks have to be completed
by yesterday'. It was the instrumental role as opposed to the
expressive role which heads of department claimed that they
could do best. Most suggested that if they had an additional
allocation of non-teaching time and less teaching, the
conflict caused by completing management tasks during lesson
time might be resolved. The empirical evidence suggested that
there was a distinct possibility that the effective accom-
plishment of instrumental roles could be an outcome, but

## A Leadership Role

their expressive roles would remain a major contributor to
the role conflict unless they were trained in the key areas
which they have admitted they found diffcult to practise.

The problems of role conflict will remain for heads of
department as long as their role has built-in role conflicts,
of leading professonal administrator, master teacher and
middle manager. However, the findings of this study showed
that the role conflict was exacerbated because heads of
department lacked training in management practice. Some of
these weaknesses were recognized by heads of department themselves, as well as being identified by departmental members
and senior management.

The transition from assistant teacher to head of department
was understood by many interviewees as a move from assistant
teacher to senior assistant teacher or master teacher rather
than to the manager of a department with assistant teacher
responsibilities. A response that

> I don't see myself (H.o.D.) as a manager ... sums up
> where I have failed to do my job ... it is to relate
> to people ...

encaspulates the attitude, lack of confidence and awareness
of the majority of heads of department at Hodson High School.
The reasons for this insecurity reflected the vagueness of
their role, in part their own personalities, and in part the
fact that the head of department role is evolving. A clear
job description which has been negotiated with heads of
department would have caused them to be aware of senior
management expectations, and for the latter to be aware of
middle manager's role conflict. An awareness of circumstances
is the first step in resolving perceived problems, and a
fundamental problem causing the master/middle manager conflict was that heads of department did not perceive themselves as middle managers.

## 8 PERCEPTIONS OF HEADS OF DEPARTMENTS' TRAINING NEEDS

## Introduction

It has clearly emerged from the findings of this study that heads of department at Hodson High School took up their posts without receiving management training. Although they survived, they still had not learned the major skills for managing their departments, even, in some cases, after eight years in post. Apart from the lack of positive direction they were able to give their departmental colleagues and, through them, the students of the school, heads of department suffered a high degree of anxiety and uncertainty because they knew that they were often ineffective as middle managers.

During interviews they shared in confidence their fears, frustrations, ignorance and perceived weaknesses which were mostly concealed beneath the cloak of professionalism and the human trait of pride. They declared in which aspects of their work they considered they needed to be trained in order to become effective and efficient. Added to this dimension, members of the senior management team, as well as departmental members, shared their perspectives where they considered heads of department could cultivate self awareness and sensitivity to other people, thereby creating a climate in which good management could prevail within the school's organization. Heads of department believed that they had been trained as teachers, and they perfected that training to become master teachers. Training was interpreted by them in terms of gaining professional credibility which in turn would give them security and confidence in their work.

'The most difficult task is handling people' was a thought expressed by all but one of the heads of department at Hodson High School, but they failed to understand that their stance as master teachers of children imposing their will caused their present unease as middle managers when dealing with adults. Negotiation was therefore the first major training need as a means of enabling them to communicate more effectively with other adults. It was manifestly obvious that heads of department were asking indirectly to learn this skill.

Based on the number of times concern was expressed by heads of department about delegation, this 'subject' also claimed a place in the training needs. Appraisal and evaluation as a means of monitoring staff professional development were major areas of concern. Change and innovation were also topics in the findings giving both departmental members and heads of department much concern, particularly in the way the latter managed planned change.

Finally, the aspiration of every head of department at Hodson High School was to build a strong departmental team and for departmental members to belong to a strong team, yet few departments experienced effective teamwork; team building, therefore, was included in the list of major training needs. This core of training needs embraced other specific areas of concern, such as staff development and curriculum development, and, lastly, the management of time (this subject was habitually used by heads of department as a reason for not being effective managers) made a sixth major training need.

## Negotiation

A concept of 'negotiation' was developed by Strauss and his

colleagues (Strauss, 1964), and has been further developed by other sociologists, for example, Goffman (1968, 1969, 1972, 1975), Barnes (1969), Hanson (1976), Woods (1983) and Hammersley (1983). This bargaining or 'negotiation' is influenced by the relative status of participants and their knowledge, and the understanding of that knowledge. This was not often apparent in the observation of departmental or informal meetings. A method of 'do me a favour' often prevailed, based on little rational thought, and sometimes a passing whim. In formal meetings, I noted frequently either an authoritative approach by heads of department towards colleagues in the process of decision-making, or they held back significant information from the meeting as a means of gaining 'the upper hand' in discussion. A process of negotiation was rarely observed.

Empirical data showed that heads of department found themselves in a catch 22 situation, that is, creating a cocoon around themselves in order to maintain a sense of security yet wishing to lead a strong departmental team, without knowing how to develop confidence in the practice of 'handling people'. In only two departments was negotiation observed and neither head of department referred to this aspect of his work as negotiation. In those two departments a climate had been created where all members of the department, the head of it included, sought to understand the activities of the department and influenced discussion on these matters.

The 'cocoon' which most heads of department created for themselves was 'woven' with 'threads' from a number of sources. They felt confident as master teachers in the classroom as they believed they had been trained for this role. The stance taken in the classroom when dealing with students was generally one of imposition, but this same attitude towards fellow professional adults did not lead to a sense of security, but one of unease as their role was challenged. A classic example was a departmental member refusing a 'delegated' task because it was not his 'job'. 'This left me floundering ...' reported the head of department; he lacked the conviction that he knew what to do as a result of his feeling 'untrained' for a middle manager's role. Evidently heads of department wanted someone to 'tell' them what to do - to train them. This conclusion additionally reflected their limited perspective of the concept of training. The declared lack of trust in departmental members should be added to the authoritative and autocratic leadership stance of the majority already referred to, for it was most apparent in their attitude towards the practice of delegation, which resulted in distancing themselves from their colleagues.

In contrast, departmental members desired discussion about issues, not only to gain information but to increase understanding. Such professional dialogues would create the possiblity of developing good working relationships with heads of department; but alleged limited availability of time often prevented these discussions. Another recurring theme throughout the study was the effect of teacher professional autonomy which had isolated colleagues, one from another, and was a 'cloak' used to conceal professional weaknesses. From time to time heads of department actually practised professional autonomy for these purposes, but they also met resistance to change and unco-operation from departmental members who also wished to claim professional autonomy.

The other major thread came to light as perceptions of organization emerged. Heads of department were functionalist in their outlook and perceived their role as a fixed position within the school's hierarchy. Together, all these factors or 'threads' caused the majority of them to be insular and lacking in sensitivity towards their colleagues, thus leaving them feeling incompetent as middle managers. Indeed, the operative word 'middle' caused many of them to think that promotion would alleviate the uncomfortable tension of feeling that they were piggy-in-the-middle between senior management on the one hand, and departmental members on the other.

# Heads of Departments' Training Needs

Through negotiation, professional bridges can be built between members of the department and between the head of department and his colleagues. The process of negotiation, 'taught me to be positive and precise', was the declared experience of just one individual at Hodson High School who had attended a Teachers' Union Representative Course on the subject of negotiation. Precision was often lacking in the process of seeking to innovate within their departments. This resulted in the frustration of departmental members and the failure of many innovations. This lack of precision was also noted in the process of delegation, resulting in misunderstandings.

It was significant that whilst the process of negotiation may result in a reduction of teachers' autonomy, this could be balanced by a positive framework for both individual and departmental development, which ironically were the aspirations of every head of department for their departmental team. The process of negotiation could also provide the means for heads of department to discover what was happening within their departments. It would also expose the strengths and weaknesses of heads of department, an issue which had remained concealed behind the cloak of professionalism; the evolving role of head of department, and the belief that they had an unreasonable allocation of time in which to exercise their role.

In analysing the empirical data it was evident that the process of negotiation would provide 'growth points' for heads of department. The majority of them felt unfulfilled in their present roles. For those few peers who did practise negotiation, job satisfaction as well as the involvement of colleagues in the department's work was apparent. This involvement led to such management practices as delegation, staff appraisal and evaluation. Indeed, the practice of negotiation would appear to be the key to other management practices so far unattained by the majority of heads of department at Hodson High School.

## Heads of Departments' Training Needs

## Delegation

In sharp contrast to negotiation the topic most discussed by
heads of department throughout the study was delegation. On
reflection it was not surprising that they found problems
with either contemplating or actually delegating tasks, since
the perceptions of their own role were far from clear to
them. In short, it was observed that the practice of delegation proved difficult for them and hence for their
departmental colleagues.

A common view expressed by the majority of heads of department was that 'Delegation is hard ... it is easier to do
it yourself ...'. Underpinning this bland and facile
statement were personal attitudes and prejudices. An attitude
prevailed that delegation could be a good idea, but they did
not have enough time in which to delegate tasks. They
considered it to be

> ... far quicker and more effective in the long term to
> do jobs yourself ...

Inevitably all management tasks will take time to implement,
but only part of the frustration of delegation was caused by
the constraint of time; the other major factors were an
apparent inability to negotiate and a lack of understanding
of people working in the school organization. It was not
surprising to find that departmental members were confused
about their head of department's expectations of them, and
they felt a sense of injustice having 'to do some of his
(H.o.D.'s) work'. On occasions some refused to accept delegated tasks, interpreting delegation as unfairly off-
loading work. This left the head of department floundering,
'What do you do when they (departmental members) say that's
not my job?'

These experiences of heads of department were indicators why
many of their peers did not pursue the practice of delegation
and that the majority of comments made about delegation were

negative, namely reasons for not delegating tasks. With this reluctance to delegate there was also little cognisance of the fact that the only way out of being constantly under pressure with day-to-day commitments was to delegate tasks to colleagues. For the heads of department who regularly delegated work, the majority of tasks lacked coherence, in the sense that their implementation tended to isolate departmental members rather than integrate them within departments. A common delegated task was that of departmental stock, ensuring that inventories were maintained and that the standard of the stock did not deteriorate in quality or quantity. The delegated tasks of one departmental mwmber were understood as

> Everyday nitty gritty ... checking on sets of books;
> keeping a check on the apparatus, though the ancillary
> staff do a very good job here; writing up the orders
> and totting up the money ... admin. of internal exams.

Individuals who received this type of delegated task became involved with departmental colleagues only when text books were misused, equipment mislaid or the stock cupboard was unbearably untidy. Indeed, few of the delegated tasks noted actually enhanced professional development, increased staff motivation, or were used as a means of integrating departmental members into a team, which were the three main reasons given by heads of department for practising delegation. From other interviews it was apparent that interviewees received pseudo tasks. For example

> My delegated work sounds grander than it really is ...
> I just prepare set lists... not an onerous task ... my
> scale post is not so much for the work which is being
> allocated ... if I had been teaching another subject
> (other than Science) others (staff in the school)
> would have been in the running (for the scale point).

Pseudo-delegation was prevalent and it resulted in isolating departmental members from their colleagues, rather than integrating members within the departmental team. In contrast,

# Heads of Departments' Training Needs

delegated responsibility for a student year group's progress within the department could give experience in co-ordinating work of other departmental members, the opportunity to evaluate a scheme of work and collate student assessments.

It was found that other delegated tasks within a school rather than a departmental responsibility created role conflict and frustration for departmental members. For example

> I suppose I ought to do more in the department ... because I have so many things to do outside the department ... the amount of time in the department is minimal ...

was the reaction of one member of staff whose graded post was given for co-ordinating a school resource. Delegated responsibilities were recognized in terms of the financial rewards of recipients and status, and the implications and process of delegation were not given high priority.

Problems of getting feedback from colleagues who received delegated tasks were caused by departmental heads' limited understanding of the process of delegation, and the lack of negotiation and consultation within that process. The 'delegating down' approach of most heads of department reflected their personal formal hierarchical understanding of an organization. In many cases the lack of accountability expected by them gave further evidence that delegation amounted to an abdication of responsibility. A departmental member reflected:

> In many ways we are left to sink or swim ... it is a matter of trial and error to see if it works ... at best you may say we are allowed to make our mistakes.

To complement this general view of delegatees, a majority of heads of department agreed that the practice of delegation was 'You delegate ... then you carry the can when things go wrong'.

# Heads of Departments' Training Needs

These views pointed to a gulf between delegator and delegatee with little evidence of there having been, or a desire for, the process of consultation, negotiation, evaluation and appraisal as part of the practice of delegation.

For the small minority of departmental heads who considered that they had mastered the art of delegation, 'The need to plan ahead before delegating tasks ...' was considered to be the key to success. It was declared that in the process of planning, the art was to match a delegated task with the delegatee. However, matching a task with a delegatee was often decided by heads of department alone and there was no attempt to negotiate an agreement between them and the departmental member. An autocratic attitude was also displayed when departmental members did not fulfil their expectations. Delegated tasks were wihdrawn from colleagues which undermined both their confidence and the credibility of the head of department in practising delegation.

> It was a scissors and paste job that wasn't
> satisfactory ... that is all he (departmental member)
> was prepared to do. I (H.o.D.) don't think he will get
> much more responsibility delegated to him; I just had
> to take this delegated task away from him ...

The result of failing on one single occasion to succeed with a delegated task culminated in departmental activities being curtailed, and the process of delegation for Rupert (departmental member) became a demotivator to his professional development.

Throughout the many references to delegation made by heads of department, senior management and departmental members, there was no overt recognition that a teaching load deployed to departmental members was a delegated task. It was assumed that teachers 'received' a specific work load, 'which was on the school timetable', and this was their lot for the ensuing academic year. The paradigm in the minds of most heads of department when considering the practice of delegation was that of a sructuralist where no real authority was delegated, but only a workload passed out to subordinates. The advantages of, and positive reasons for, delegation were yet to be grasped by the majority of heads of department, and the skills of this particular management practice required.

A head of department who had considered the many comments of members of staff which could possibly be levelled against him, used the phrase: 'I could do their (H.o.D.) job with my eyes shut', as the main reason for delegation. He sought to give departmental members an appreciation of the role of head of department and as a means of developing a strong departmental and individual staff development.

> Delegation is important in making other members of the
> department involved (in the work of the department).
> It is important that all members are able to cope with
> and have expectations of responsibility for their
> future career and to feel part of the department.

In this department every member was aware, in varying degrees, of the delegated responsibilities of colleagues, and regular meetings were used as a forum in which feedback was received from members. Here the head of department was not isolated from the departmental team. Such a system aided the process of departmental communication, and firmly placed the process of delegation on a departmental plane with the head of it as the co-ordinator of the tasks delegated. Additional reasons for delegation were expessed by the same head of department:

> Delegation has other spin-offs ... it is a means of
> producing confidence boosters ... it also gives you
> the opportunity to appraise work and say 'thank you'.

This quotation presented a positive attitude towards the practice of delegation, involving both training and development, and also acting as a means of giving praise for the successful completion of tasks. Indeed such an approach to the process of delegation created a framework in which staff appraisal could take place.

During this study it was noted that delegation had both functional and dysfunctional consequences, and this highlighted the fact that there was an informal risk which delegators must take. Although the process of delegation provided the opportunity for co-operation and inter-dependence amongst colleagues, the dilemma between meeting individual needs and departmental demands, a potential source of conflict, was a reality for every delegator. It was also clear that where delegation did not occur a barrier was created between the head of department and his departmental colleagues, thus suggesting that delegation was a means of enhancing rather than threatening a head of department's role. Put another way, delegation was a method of getting the most out of both a head of department and his team, for it could enable a head of department not only to devote time to other issues, but also be a means of management development.

The art of delegation appears to lie in an organization in which the individual may obtain optimum expression. The paradigm in which this is perceived accepts delegation as a growth process, similar to that expressed about the practice of negotiation where understanding and insights are gained by both delegator and delegatee. This management skill, like that of negotiation, can create the climate in which ev-aluation, staff appraisal, innovation and teamwork may develop, the reticence of heads of department to practise delegation may well be related to their attitude of opting out of acceptng the role of staff developer. Furthermore an attitude which prevailed amongst heads of department that departmental responsibilities ought not to be delegated to junior teachers not holding posts of responsibility created an unnecessary barrier between colleagues.

Training in the practice of delegation could cause heads of department to reflect upon these issues, and balance the

## Heads of Departments' Training Needs

advantages and disadvantages of delegation for individual departmental members themselves and the whole department. Certainly the process of delegation could bring heads of department into a close working relationship with colleagues, an experience which was frequently only a superficial reality for them. The practice of delegation was a much under-rated management skill.

## Staff Appraisal and Evaluation

Akin to the relationship of the subjects 'Change' and 'Innovation', Appraisal and Evaluation are subjects which are integrally inter-related in management practice. For ease of presentation, staff appraisal is considered first.

The empirical data showed that heads of department thought that the practice of staff appraisal could be a means of creating positive professional dialogue between themselves and their departmental members. It was also evident that it could be an effective means of communicating departmental business to senior management. A further purpose identified by a minority of heads of department was that it could be a vehicle for giving guidance to colleagues, but for the majority a framework in which criticism, often thought to be negative, could be levelled against staff.

> Weeding people out ... people are allowed to just
> muddle along without being sorted out.

However, heads of department were vague in their philosophy of staff appraisal, and openly admitted that they lacked the skills to practise staff appraisal.

The great majority of departmental members at Hodson High School lacked the experience of being party to negotiated departmental aims and objectives or personal departmental targets to be achieved during an academic year. Such experience, knowledge and expectations on the part of the departmental members and the head of department could have given both parties a framework in which staff appraisal might occur. In other words, departmental members lacked role expectation, and heads of department lacked the skills and knowledge of making staff appraisal a reality for them. Indeed, effective departmental delegation could have created the forum in which meaningful staff appraisal occurred. It was also significant to note that heads of department were unaware of the growing body of literature on staff appraisal, although some of them showed that they had a nodding acquaintance with staff appraisal, based on "Times Educational Supplement" articles.

During this study the topic of staff appraisal was raised by interviewees when discussing praise and/or criticism of staff. All members of staff generally agreed that 'It is nice to be praised and recognized for what you do (well)', and that staff appraisal was perceived by many departmental members as a method of identifying good practice. Criticism was often made of senior management by both heads of department and departmental members that they were unaware of staff teaching and management practices.

> The job of a middle manager is to train probationers
> and to be checked on by senior management ... if you
> have done it well then you should be told so. Praise
> and criticism must be given to individuals ... nobody
> knows where they are going until this happens.

The response of senior management to the criticism that they did not find out about good professional practice was to criticize heads of department who failed to inform them

> I value it when a head of department tells me that
> so-and-so is doing well. Sometimes they (H.o.D's)
> think I automatically know these things ...

was the reaction of the headteacher. In the minds of senior management their expectations of middle managers were clear;

# Heads of Departments' Training Needs

that they should be appraisers of departmental members and should combine this role with 'keeping a tight rein on things'. This phrase reflects the concern of senior management that heads of department found much difficulty in managing departmental members. The end result was that heads of department opted out of many of their responsibilities, not wishing to be staff developers, delegators, evaluators or appraisers and were content to relay anecdotal data about colleagues to senior management which was often based on speculation. In fairness to departmental heads, however, they received no guidance or training on the method of appraising colleagues nor were they required to practise any form of staff appraisal.

By far the greatest concern from both probationary teachers and senior management about an aspect of appraising staff focussed on the preparation and writing of probationary teachers' reports. Senior management expressed the general view that the process of appraising colleagues in their probationary period of service was 'hit and miss'. Probationary teachers shared their anxieties, stating that few heads of department made classroom observation of their teaching. They chose to make cursory visits to classrooms on a variety of pretexts.

> ... he (H.o.D.) never sat in on a lesson; he used to pop in a lot ... would come in for a blackboard rubber or something like that ... always unobtrusive ...

Another person related

> Peter (H.o.D.) was often outside and he told me he knew what was going on without coming in ... this didn't help too much ... it was a matter of teaching by proxy ... it would have been better if he had come in and given guidance on the work level expected ... guidance on marking ... I felt as though I was on trial which was a little unfortunate to say the least.

# Heads of Departments' Training Needs

First hand knowledge of probationary teachers' classroom performance was desired, followed by positive criticism which would support the teacher at the beginning of his professional career. Ignorance about the results of appraisal resulted in assumptons based on silence. Another area of criticism was that heads of department were bland in their comments, suggesting that they did not know how to appraise staff and that they lacked confidence to do the work. Not only probationary teachers but many teachers at Hodson High School, including experienced teachers, would have welcomed staff appraisal as a means of guidance for:

> Everyone needs to know where they are going ... I
> needed a proper supply of materials in adequate time
> to prepare lessons ... the head of department must
> make sure that people in my position (senior member of
> staff) are equipped and not make the assumption that
> if all is quiet, all is well. If I'm making a mess of
> things I'm not going to broadcast it ... my head of
> department must treat me a a probationer ... coming
> into lessons; he must take the initiative ... general
> discussion about progress is needed.

It was most significant to learn what happened when members did not receive help from their head of department, and were not prepared to ask for support.

> I would like support there (from head of department).
> but haven't got it, so I go on my own and steer clear
> of things I'm not sure of....

Their reaction was not an isolated case resulting in the quality of the educative process being inhibited and the quality of work minimized.

Whilst on the one hand there was a body of criticism about heads of department not appraising classroom performance, it was acknowledged that for most heads of department their teaching commitment did not readily present an opportunity to

140

exercise this professional practice. 'He (the H.o.D.) was always teaching when I was', frequently occurred in conversation.

The general attitude of most heads of department towards staff appraisal was the same as their approach towards delegation:

> Appraisal is a good idea... but where do you find the
> time to do this sort of thing.

Another area of concern expressed was: 'How do you measure success?', which highlighted a fundamental issue of evaluation techniques. Also subsumed within their concern of 'measuring the success' of colleagues, was confusion about the implications of staff appraisal. In the succinct words of one head of department, 'easier said than done'. Indeed this confusion undermined the confidence of most heads of department who openly admitted that they found difficulty in managing people and, '...it is the fear of not being liked'. How much more this proved to be a problem to heads of department as they had no perceived paradigm in which the concept of staff appraisal could operate.

Most heads of department were autocratic in their leadership style and were structuralists in their understanding of organizations. This stance was reflected in their predominant interpretation of staff appraisal as a means of criticizing colleagues, often in a negative and authoritarian manner. However, the desire of heads of department to be efficient and effective was noted throughout interviews, and was expressed in such ways as:

> I would like some training in the things I am
> responsible for: I then can give my staff the security
> to know what should be done, and what I know is good,
> and then they will feel a sense that the advice I give
> is good.

## Heads of Departments' Training Needs

Whilst the logic of this quotation could be considered suspect, the spirit in which the view was expressed was clear; namely the desire to solve identified departmental problems but with an autocratic style of management. This stance was not likely to contribute greatly towards solving the problems of irregular professional dialogue or what was termed 'feedback', as it frequently created resentment amongst departmental members. A realization by some heads of department of these circumstances caused them to seek alternative methods of 'taking people to task' in order to rectify departmental problems. It was clear that the majority of heads of department wished to work closely with departmental members, but they did not know how to set about building up professional working relationships with them.

The skills of interviewing and counselling were perceived by many heads of department as a vital omission from their experience and training.

> I still don't know how to interview...I don't really
> have a clue how to set about asking the right sort of
> questions...

was a reaction by a head of department who had been involved with many staff appointments. Arising from the topic of interviewing candidates for teaching posts, there was the desire to counsel departmental colleagues.

> I(H.o.D) get on well with Joe (departmental member)
> who was just waiting for me to go. I tried to intimate
> that he would not get the job (H.o.D.), but I didn't
> sit down and say, 'You won't get it'...I don't know
> how to...

The experience cited by another head of department also highlighted this issue.

> How can you tell a man approaching forty (years of
> age) that he won't go any further...we have told

> young staff that they won't get head of department
> jobs...very difficult for a younger person (H.o.D)
> telling an older man why his career isn't going
> places.

Such was the concern of heads of department wishing to take
an active part in the professional development of departmental colleagues, but not feeling confident to perform
this role. Within the context of staff appraisal counselling
skills were essential in dealing with staff problems:
weaknesses as well as 'A prominent thing in this school
(Hodson High School) that people get "burnt out"...' was a
cry from the heart. This signalled a danger to guard against
with a highly committed and motivated staff who were unable
to manage, affecting their staff, time and resources.

A realization that staff appraisal can be an on-going process
of building up professional working relationships and not
confined to an annual interview 'to weed out weak teachers'
could assist heads of department in their understanding of a
process of staff appraisal, and their own role as staff
developer. It has already been noted that they did not
perceive themselves as staff developers, although they wished
to support colleagues who experienced difficulties. Their
reasons for not wishing to accept this role were that they
did not have the time to fulfil such a role; they did not
have the opportunity to identify staff development needs;
they thought departmental members were capable of identifying
their own staff development needs, and there was an unease
and in some cases fear at the prospect of observing
colleagues teaching in their classroom. However, the
empirical data clearly showed that departmental members, both
experienced and inexperienced, desired guidance and reassurance from their head of department.

For the majority of heads of department their interpretation
of staff appraisal gave emphasis to appraisal performance
highlighting an inspectorial role, as opposed to a

professional review with an emphasis on colleagues and fellow professionals in dialogue about matters of mutual concern.

The problem of managing time in which appraisal takes place will remain a reality for heads of department as staff appraisal will take much time. However, the fact that many heads of department already perceived the benefits of staff appraisal, augured well for their own job satisfaction and potential improvement in a range of management skills. Indeed, staff appraisal, a new and tender plant in many schools, required careful nurturing and an expertise in a number of management skills which most heads of department at Hodson High School lacked such as counselling, negotiation and evaluation, the next subject to be considered.

As the management practice of staff appraisal may lead to self-justification rather than genuine self-reflection (see Rodger, 1983), so the practice of evaluation may result in reinforcing mediocrity (see Nuttall, 1981). Such results are always possible when human beings are involved in these management practices, particularly if they are unsure of themselves, lacking in confidence and have a fixation about an admission of failure.

Although the majority of heads of department claimed directly or indirectly not to know about evaluation techniques, it was interesting to note that all without exception perceived that evaluation was about power and control over departmental affairs. There was also a realization amongst the majority of them that the practice of evaluation should be an integral part of their work, but they accepted that evaluation was rarely a reality.

> Evaluation ... to sit back and think...did anything go
> wrong and why...I think that you should evaluate your
> work all the time...but it doesn't get done.

Most heads of department felt uncomfortable when the topic of evaluation was discussed with me which manifested both their

144

# Heads of Departments' Training Needs

limited knowledge of the literature on this subject and the ways of setting about evaluating departmental activities.

> I do not feel at all pleased with evaluation ... (but) ... there's only twenty four hours in the day ...

was not an uncommon reaction to the subject of evaluation. This vagueness of approach was communicated through many other comments such as

> If you follow it (the department's scheme of work) through and evaluate it, then you get a more creative approach ...,

but there were no clear messages of methodology to be used in evaluating a scheme of work and the 'if' was not an enthusiastic possibility, Another bland response was:

> Some departments are not keen on analysing their curriculum and evaluating schemes of work ...,

again suggesting that evaluation was not considered to be an important practice and was rarely used.

The evidence from departmental members, senior management and heads of department themselves revealed that the well worn phrase: 'I haven't time to evaluate...' was used as an excuse for incompetence. This phrase also revealed the low priority given to the practice of evaluation by interviewees and in turn displayed the limited use they foresaw in completing evaluation exercises on departmental planning. Some heads of department actually shared in confidence:

> I don't think ... if I'm honest ... that I ever thought much about the evaluation of work.

Two main reasons were noted why heads of department rarely practised evaluation. The first reason was the practice of professional autonomy which cloaked their ignorance. Phrases frequently used by interviewees in connection with evaluation were, 'I'm sure that I'm on the right lines', or 'I'm confident that we're (the department) going in the right direction'. These reactions gave an air of confidence, but were also a signal to members of the role set not to pry and enquire too deeply into the work of the department; a defence mechanism to avoid discussion about the subject of evalua- tion. The other reason was that members of staff were not required to be accountable for their work. If heads of department and/or departmental members were held accountable for their professional activities, particularly within the context of a staff appraisal system, then the practice of evaluation would more likely have become a reality than in the present circumstances where there was much evidence of industry, but it lacked clear direction and accountability.

It was also found that the concept of evaluation was often confused in the minds of heads of department with assessment. 'Evaluation' was a term often used as being synonymous with the term 'Assessment'. This was another indicator high- lighting the limited understanding of heads of department about this subject. There was also little knowledge, that no one method of evaluating educational activities was suitable for all situations. To take, for example, Scrivens' (1967) "Classifying Evaluation Designs": heads of department would realize the distinction between the goal of evaluation - its 'worth' - and the roles of evaluation - the reasons and circumstances for needing to know the 'worth'. Evaluation tech- niques could be considered from many sources: for example, the 'illuminative', (Parlett and Hamilton, 1972) or 'responsive', (Stake, 1980) model which acknowledged the com- plexity of educational settings and the unintended con- sequences of curriculum programmes (Steadman in McCormick, 1982, Tawney, 1976 or Thomas in Hughes et al, 1985). But the major requirement for most heads of department was to grow in confidence in order to accept that evaluation is a service industry and not designed to be a threat to their professional status and that of their colleagues.

# Heads of Departments' Training Needs

> How do you know whether you are effective...people
> (departmental members) have suggested that I wasn't
> effective...I found this depressing and devastating...

Evaluation practised as a departmental activity could become
an integral part of an INSET programme, meeting not only the
needs of heads of department but also the declared needs of
departmental members. To achieve such practices heads of
department required training in the skills and process of
evaluation.

Frequently a crisis marked a problem rather than the process
of evaluation giving an indicator of departmental difficulties to a head of department. It was realized that
evaluation could give reassurance to individual departmental
members as well as to a whole department, but heads of
department chose to drift through their work not seeking
assistance from their super-ordinates or from their own
personal reading. These circumstances reflected the tremend-
ous fear, that an admission of ignorance or incompetence
could jeopardize the chances of promotion for them. It also
emphasized the deeply ingrained false assumptions within the
teaching profession that basic skills and knowledge such as
evaluation techniques and design had been acquired and were
practised by middle managers.

A summary of the results of heads of department who failed to
practise evaluation was encapsulated in the terse words of
one of their number:

> People haven't grown professionally 'cos they have
> never been caused to evaluate. This has bred arrogance
> and I'm doing O.K.

This personal view pervaded the empirical data where
departmental heads gave false impressions of confidence and
competence, and as such was a stmbling block to any training
which could be provided for them. The effective practice of

147

evaluation as an integral part of staff appraisal could have sharpened the focus of the work of both heads of department and their departmental members, but the 'top-down' autocratic approach taken by most heads of department was not likely to produce positive outcomes. Indeed, an improved understanding about the subject of evaluation could contribute very much to departmental heads' effectiveness as middle managers and service other management practices such as delegation and team building as well as staff appraisal.

## Change and Innovation

The management of change and the practice of innovation are inter-related and were two subjects deeply reflected in the ethos and environment of Hodson High School. Over a period of eight years since its inauguration heads of department and departmental members at the school experienced continuous change and numerous innovations: some inevitable as the student roll grew, but most as the school curriculum evolved. Other changes and innovations were the result of heads of department seeking to be in the vanguard of curriculum development as a means of gaining promotion and senior management wishing to create a vibrant school environment.

It was apparent that heads of department did not fully understand nor had they studied 'change' or 'innovation'. They had little or no awareness of the vast literature on these subjects, which left many of them in a situation of 'trial and error', lurching from one innovation to another and eventually after eight years of working in this environment, feeling, by their own admission, 'burnt out'. Since heads of department had not studied the management of change but knew from personal experience how difficult it was to manage change, they were at the mercy of their own anxieties and enthusiasm. Often this resulted in indecisive situations in their departments, as aptly described by one departmental member: 'We are all in a whirlwind job ... nobody knows what's going to happen next ...'.

## Heads of Departments' Training Needs

A lack of consultation with departmental members prevented the opportunity of understanding a process of change or the philosophy and content of an innovation. A head of department admitted that as pressures built up they did not communicate. In fact, the omission to consult colleagues about innovations cloaked the ignorance of heads of department on the management of change, but also highlighted their preferred style of leadership of imposition on, as opposed to negotiation with, colleagues. Other reactions of departmental members to change and innovation varied from person to person, but their common views were significant. Many teachers shared their anxieties and bewilderment for:

> Nothing stands still here ... what is new now is supposed to be good ... for the past six years there's been change, accepting it as a norm ... it's amazing how much pressure this puts on people. A fault of ours is that we change too readily ... nothing stands still here ... there's too much trial and error with curriculum development.

Clearly the many curriculum development initiatives experienced by departmental staff were not 'a professional activity, consciously and deliberately carried out by teachers and others' (D.E.S., 1985a), and therefore often met with an inevitable 'tissue rejection' (Hoyle, 1970).

An appreciation by heads of department of the complexity of the concept of innovation could have given them greater awareness of the crucial periods of preparation and 'after care' following an innovation. Insufficient time was taken by the great majority of heads of department carefully to plan resources, accommodation and the process of innovation, particularly from the human perspective where it has already been noted there was anxiety in exploring new areas of knowledge and skills. The importance of planning the use of time, resources and skills, such as problem-solving skills, by their absence, were not considered by most heads of department to be important in the 'after care' period following the initial period of implementation, in order to achieve an effective innovation.

Many heads of department were unaware of what was endemic in their departmental organization into which a specific innovation was to be implemented. Indeed, often innovations were attempted by merely 'planting' ideas and concepts from outside the departmental context. The process of innovation had a low priority compared with the value given to the subject to be innovated. Together, heads of department and departmental members failed to diagnose and understand growth points in the organization in which planned change could happen. A conclusion made after reflection by some heads of department and departmental members was that enthusiasm for change-seeking to cause vibrance in a department was no substitute for careful planning and consultation. Some heads of department admitted that they would have liked more guidance from senior colleagues when seeking to control change, and many of the 'crisis situations' shared with me were related either directly or indirectly with innovation and change.

Effective management of change and innovation would involve management skills which will be and have already been discussed in this and the previous chapters. The expertise or lack of expertise of heads of department in such skills affected the adoption and implementation of innovations and management of change. Taking selective pieces of literature on innovation and change could assist heads of department in being reflective on their own particular needs. For example, Gross (1971) described the fate of one innovation, highlighting the fact that the school's director failed to plan for problems which teachers might encounter, nor did he provide for feedback during the process of the innovation. This description was an identical experience to that described by many departmental members at Hodson High School: the attitude of many heads of department reflected those of the school's director. The initial stages of an innovation always involve anxiety and uncertainty for participants

# Heads of Departments' Training Needs

(Fullan, 1985): this particular management task was often ignored by the majority of heads of department in the study, and colleagues were expected to 'rise to the occasion' as true professionals.

An awareness of the strategies for innovation such as the typology presented by Chin and Benne (1969) could also assist self-reflection amongst heads of department. However, in using literature care is needed to translate theory into practice, an assumption not to be taken for granted (Wabane, 1985). For example, the 'Empirical - Rational' strategy is perceived in a vacuum and fails to take into account attitudes and values that already exist amongst teachers.

Undoubtedly, heads of department in the study lacked diagnostic skills to unravel the problems and priorities created by innovations. Another perceived need was the ability to monitor and control the process and progress of change. On this particular issue, Havelock's (1969) classification of knowledge dissemination could cause heads of department self-reflection. From the models offered by Havelock, the social interaction model mirrored the Hodson High School experience where knowledge was disseminated through informal contact, but unfortunately this process tended to be unplanned, leaving to chance people's attitudes to change. Again, the consequences of these models must never assume, as heads of department frequently did, that departmental members are passive, for there are political implications for coping with various individual interests.

Finally, planned change required a great deal of expertise, and was not a simplistic exercise as assumed by many heads of department. Co-operation and adaptability of departmental members and heads of department was needed for planned change to be achieved. Heads of department in particular have a crucial role in controlling change, but the attitudes displayed towards people and their perception of organizations did not present the ideal circumstances for successful planned change. Perhaps one of the critical ways

of aiding heads of department to increase their self awareness was through well developed teamwork, the next topic for
consideration, but the responsibility that all persons
involved in a planned change understands the content and
process of that change remained with the head of department.

## Team Building

Without exception the desire of every head of department at
Hodson High School was to create and maintain an efficient
team of teachers, but few realized their ambition.

'Stimulating learning from each other brings us together...I
would like the whole team to be as strong as me...' was not
an uncommon aspiration of heads of department. The reality of
creating a strong team of teachers in a department was
accepted as a sensitive task. Another head of department
said:

> I try to get each person to be a specialist and we can
> learn from each other which helps to develop good
> relationships...there is also then an opportunity to
> give praise...we all like a pat on the back.

So much for the idealism of the heads of department! But a
strong counter thrust of comments and opinions was also
expressed:

> I wanted to consult and create a team ... but that was
> a fool's paradise for me...as you know, I have to take
> responsibility and make decisions ... I have to carry
> the can ...

and another, not unfamiliar perspective: 'You don't go over
things together 'cos there's no spare time ...'

Indeed, heads of department found that in seeking to create a
balanced and coherent team of professional teachers was a

# Heads of Departments' Training Needs

more difficult business than was commonly realized. From observation and discussion with departmental members much evidence was found to suggest that commitment to the departmental team was less vigorous than it might have been because members were unsure and in some cases unaware of departmental policy.

The absence of agreed departmental objectives left members without a common goal upon which to focus and work towards. It was also found that little time was used to share problems of mutual concern with departmental members and to plan departmental strategies. A lack of time was purported to be a major reason for heads of department failing to delegate tasks, a process which could aid a team spirit amongst colleagues. Another factor militating against teamwork was that many departmental members claimed the right of professional autonomy as a means of taking independent decisions regardless of the views and activities of other members of the department.

These findings did not augur well for heads of department to create strong departmental teams. Underpinning the management problems in team building, experienced by the majority of heads of department, were their poor attitudes and limited understanding about people and organizations already discussed in the previous chapter. A declared lack of tryst in colleagues was in essence an admission that they did not wish or they found difficulty in forfeiting control over their colleagues. Indeed, trust between team members is the bedrock upon which interpersoal skills may develop, and a means of creating a cohesive team where people are recognized as having different personalities, attitudes, strengths and weaknesses. The autocratic style of leadership practised by the majority of heads of department did not enhance an environment where teamwork could develop, as departmental members often resented this leadership style. A telling remark from one head of department that 'I've had to learn to deal with colleagues because I'm dependent upon them ...' was a realization which dawned after six years in post. Another

# Heads of Departments' Training Needs

interviewee described in vivid terms his experience of
confrontations he had with members of his department, and
went on to say:

> I didn't really consider the role of the head of
> department...how very necessary it is to consult with
> people ...taking them into account is quite a delicate
> exercise ...

The taken-for-granted responsibilities of heads of department
which were not attempted or poorly achieved by them were ill-
uminating.

Almost every departmental team at Hodson High School had a
senior member of staff working in it or a teacher of equivalent status to a head of department. It has already been
noted that the hierarchical perspectives of most heads of
department caused them much difficulty in dealing with these
colleagues. Their lack of negotiating skills came into sharp
focus when they were obliged to deal with either members of
their peer group who worked in their department, those
colleagues who were chronologically older than themselves or
their super-ordinates. In the majority of these situations
heads of department avoided issues and chose to ignore
problems and difficulties. For example:

> My department is top-heavy ... is the highest paid
> department in the Authority ... our department lacks
> cohesion ... there are so many people whose
> administrative demands are elsewhere ... we have
> meetings with a hard core (of those not of equal or
> superior status to the H.o.D.) then there are memos
> flying around to update the rest ...

This reflected the feelings of one frustrated head of
department who was unable to guarantee a full attendance of
staff at departmental meetings. The possibilities therefore
of developing teamwork by integrating these colleagues into a
department were slim. Another problem militating against the

## Heads of Departments' Training Needs

development of a strong departmental team was that the
majority of departments had some members with allegiance to
more than one department. The deployment of these staff did
not enhance possibilities of creating a coherent team. This
area of conflict was acutely acknowledged by heads of
department but was often accentuated by their negative
attitudes, for there was no evidence that they sought to
resolve these problems, only to bemoan the fact.

## Opportunities for Team Building

Appraisal and evaluation have already been referred to and in
particular evaluation practised as a co-operative exercise
providing a positive framework for departmental/team development but at the same time reducing teachers' autonomy. It is
important to note that this latter factor - teacher
professional autonomy - was found to be a strong negative
force, inhibiting team building. The process of planned
change also presented heads of department with the opportunity for team building, but it has been shown that insufficient time was taken to involve colleagues in planning
innovations and in consideration given to the needs of
individual members anxious about change. The lack of
negotiation by heads of department failed to present an essential element in team building in the process of causing
agreement or compromise amongst departmental members. The end
remit was often a fragmented department of individual members
lacking a sense of team identity. For those who delegated
responsibilities to departmental members, the majority of
such tasks caused members to be isolated within the department. I noted that most heads of department failed to
delegate departmental business to junior members of staff who
did not expect to be involved in departmental activities
other than classroom teaching which militated against
developing a team spirit. Furthermore, the fact that the vast
majority of departmental members' time was used in classroom
teaching and that the outcome of this work was not recognized
as a fundamental part of the department's work, the potential

# Heads of Departments' Training Needs

for team building was again minimized.

A great deal has been noted already in these findings about heads of department using much energy in defending their departmental boundaries, and thereby isolating their departments from other departments. John Donne's phrase 'No man is an island' equally applied to the departmental team and appeared to be a hard lesson for most heads of department and departmental members to learn. Forging links with other departments in the school could generate team work particularly if the ethos had been created in departments where team work was being developed. Such activities would also give heads of department, in their roles as curriculum leaders, an insight into an all-school curriculum policy, which was lacking at Hodson High School.

In this study there was frequently a misconception on the part of senior management and some heads of department that increased information led automatically to greater understanding and better relationships with people. Often the reverse seemed to be true, for most people chose 'that which suited his own purpose' rather than that of the departmental team. Creating a team mentality amongst departmental members was a subject not actively considered by many heads of department, nor were methods of creating such a mentality evident, such as the regular monitoring of the department's progress by the departmental team. It was also assumed by senior management and many heads of department that departmental meetings created the forum in which team building operated, but this was not the case. 'Lots of meetings are held for the sake of meetings ...' was the attitude of many staff members, and so this raised the issues of the involvement of departmental members in meetings, the topics discussed, and the skills of the chairman in conducting the meeting. Frequently a concern was expressed that: 'They (the meetings) are usually about examinations and good ideas. I don't like them, especially when they don't get anywhere ...'

## Heads of Departments' Training Needs

The observation of departmental meetings showed that agenda items and departmental discussions were rarely used as means to create team building situations. For example:

> Anybody can express views ... to discuss any subject
> ... I suppose I chair these meetings ... We do not
> have an agenda as such, but I make a list so we know
> what we are going to talk about ...

It was not surprising therefore that departmental business often caused division with teams rather than a coherence.

However, I did attend some effective meetings where people came prepared to participate in the meetings.

> You (departmental members) know you've got to give
> your bit ... there's a lot of simple things achieved
> ... time is well spent; we are not allowed to waffle
> ...

In such meetings the head of department had learned the skills of planning and chairmanship but this was not the norm amongst his peers. It is a truism that a team mentality is often 'caught' as a result of planned co-operative activities, and it was significant to record that those few departments with strong teams were involved in much group work with an emphasis on working together rather than an over-emphasis on discussion. Good departmental organization was considered to be an essential factor in the process of integrating colleagues into a team, particularly the probationary teacher:

> My (probationary teacher) first year was a happy one.
> The department is highly organized; everybody knows
> what everybody else is doing; schemes of work are
> excellent, and that is what has made my work so easy
> as I have never had to devise schemes of work. All I
> have had to do is to devise how to teach. On teaching
> practice (as a student teacher) you worked in

isolation. You never fear in the department (here)
that you are on your own ... there is very much a
whole department feeling ...

This description of life in a department by a young teacher
was echoed by an experienced teacher saying:

Comeraderie has been created ... there's an
expectation within the department ... you're always
welcome into one another's lessons ... The head of
department creates an environment in which the team
may develop ... However, it is important to have
freedom (as an individual) to do what you can do ...

The latter phrase was a significant view which highlighted
the role of the individual within the team who did not wish
to be over-organized. Nevertheless, the individual concerned
realized the significance of being a team member.

Good lines of communication within a department where feedback between members regularly occurred was another subject
which created much concern for many departmental members.

'Things happen in the department and I only pick them up a
few days before they happen, or sometimes after the event
...' was not an uncommon example of a departmental member not
feeling part of a team. Effective communications were desired
to develop a sense of identity with a department as well as
developing individuals within their teams. A perceived lack
of accountability structure blurred the lines of communications between heads of department and their colleagues and
caused disquiet amongst departmental members.

Possibly the greatest obstacle to team building was the
assumption made by most heads of department that they
automatically had a team created because a department was a
reality, albeit in name only. This may seem a harsh statement
to make, but it is made in the context of hearing such

# Heads of Departments' Training Needs

platitudes as 'It is good to involve others' (departmental members), without qualifying why or how that involvement should occur. To give another example of a head of a small department explaining the work of his department:

> There is little need for formality when dealing with departmental business. There's just two of us ... we split things down the middle ... and decisions to be made ... well they make themselves. We meet ... there's not the business to warrant it ... we meet informally in the staff room, or as I pass through the classroom ...

The views of departmental members did not tally with those of their heads of department for they wished to be involved in departmental matters. In reality many heads of department were experiencing what one of their peer group admitted in interview: 'None of us has been trained to be a head of department ... so we're setting up a team by instinct ...' Team work was desired by all heads of department but the fact remained: team work was not an automatic response of a group of people known as a department. It had to be managed and the majority majority of heads of department at Hodson High School failed in their aspired team building five main inter-related reasons. First, there was poor provision for a team building environment, and second, a lack of realization by the majority of heads of department that team work occurred by actually sharing tasks and responsibilities.


# Time Management

Heads of department at Hodson High School had on average a teaching commitment for eighty per cent of the school time-table, and during interview sessions they frequently complained of inadequate time in which to fulfil their roles satisfactorily. A similar allocation of teaching was the norm for heads of department in another L.E.A., and an H.M.I. team reporting on this Authority thought this was insufficient

# Heads of Departments' Training Needs

time for monitoring the work of departments, supervising the work of other teachers and planning and bringing about new developments. (D.E.S., 1984b) The argument put forward by many heads of department that 'We should have a lighter teaching load ... too much is expected of us ... we have an impossible job ...' would seem to be justified.

The senior management of Hodson High School and the L.E.A.'s role expectations of heads of department appeared to me to be unreasonable in allocating only twenty per cent non-teaching time in which to fulfil middle management tasks. This was in marked contrast to the experience of an interviewee in the pilot study who spoke of an exchange in a Canadian school. Heads of department had a written contract: a fifty per cent teaching commitment and an assured fifty per cent of their school timetable designated for managerial tasks. In contrast, in England and Wales, a vaguely defined teachers' agreement following the Houghton Report of 1974 left teaching, administrative and managerial work to the professional conscience of individual heads of department. In other words there was an assumption that middle management practice will often occur outside normal school hours, but this created genine problems. For example, classroom appraisal could take place only during school sessions when heads of department were often teaching and they were not available to observe a colleague teaching. Now that the government is introducing a contract for teachers, the first of its kind in the history of the teaching profession, requiring them to fulfil up to 1,265 hours every academic year, it still has no clear contractual obligations for heads of department. To ensure a realistic outcome from a middle manager's role a reasonable allocation of time would need to be allocated to post holders in which they could manage and supervise the work of their departments.

The major need of the majority of heads of department apparent in this study was to develop self awareness of their present use of time. A fundamental weakness noted in many aspects of their work was the lack of planning which took

160

place. In a few cases they recognized this weakness, and a fairly new head of department, feeling under extreme pressure, shared his experiences, not with senior management, but with a friend of similar age who had just become a manager of a small High Street Building Society Office. He recalled that the friend, within the first month in post, had received professional advice and training on the use of a "Time Planner". 'Why didn't I receive similar support?' was the head of department's query.

For many heads of department, coping with crisis became a way of life as they either failed to plan adequately their work or allowed themselves to be distracted from the tasks in hand. The empirical data showed that they needed to learn how to prioritize their tasks rather than try to move simultaneously on too many fronts and become bogged down in too many activities. Key departmental objectives which were not apparent would have reflected the head of department's priorities. Much use of their time was a result of departmental members not having clear expectations of their role. Negotiated job descriptions and target setting in the short term would have saved much time in the medium term for them. Both exercises would have given departmental members clear expectations for the use of their own time and would have saved unnecessary consultation with the departmental head, a thing which I frequently observed in the staffroom.

Improved management skills would have also utilized time more meaningfully, for example, effective delegation and negotiation, but heads of department needed to learn to create baffles in order to complete planned tasks in a limited period of time. The majority used the staffroom rather than their departmental offices to carry out departmental business, thus exposing themselves to constant interruptions and failure to make the greatest use of time. It was also observed that popularity amongst colleagues was often confused for the term 'support'. To say 'no' was anathema to them:

161

# Heads of Departments' Training Needs

> We take too much on and what suffers is preparation,
> but more importantly the marking and teachng ... over
> the year lateness (in arriving punctually for lessons)
> amounts to a fair number of lessons ...

Training to alert heads of department to their use or abuse
of time would help them to become not only effective, but in
the process would teach them the significance of other
managerial skills, for example, the chairing of meetings and
ensuring that matters were followed through after the
meeting. The respect for time and the acknowledgement of its
value as a resource in which activities happened or did not
happen was an essential realization for all heads of
department. Rather than catalogue the management tasks which
could not be achieved in time, the heads of department of
Hodson High Schol could well have logged their effective use
of limited time, and a list of 'Time Stealers', those
unplanned activities which absorbed management and teaching
time.

It has been established that heads of department were given
inadequate time to fulfil the role expectations of senior
management and the L.E.A., but the reason for insufficient
time was frequently used by heads of department to conceal
their management incompetence in a range of skills. The
majority of heads of department were poor managers of time
and required training in these skills, particularly as this
affected their clasroom practice, as management tasks were
often carried out when they should have been teaching
students. Indeed, the management of time is an essential
skill through which other management practices could occur.

# 9 CONCLUSIONS

Three significant factors present a backdrop against which the training needs of heads of department have come to the fore: their evolving role, appointment of middle managers, and professional autonomy and training.

## The Evolving Role

An historical perspective of the role of head of department highlighted both the lack of role definition and the evolving nature of the role. In a decentralized educational system with no specific contractual duties laid down for heads of department, their role varied from school to school, dependent upon the headteacher's and department head's interpretation of it. The Burnham Agreement of 1956 created for the first time the opportunity for L.E.A.s and subsequently headteachers to give financial responsibility allowances to heads of department. This also gave the L.E.A.s and schools the opportunity to create a clear role definition, but this has not emerged. However, throughout the period of three decades, 1956 to 1986, and reflected in the G.C.S.E. individual Subject Guides for Teachers (O.U. Press, 1986), a common view has been held that heads of department are master teachers. But an assumption found in the D.E.S. literature was that heads of department are also middle managers (see, for example, D.E.S., 1977a, 1979, 1983a, 1985a). It was in

163

# Conclusions

this latter aspect of the role that there was a particular lack of clarity and understanding.

The master teacher and middle manager role conflict put into sharp focus training needs of heads of department as middle managers which had previously been blurred due to this e-volving role. To meet the demands of curricular and examination reforms, the role of head of department may well need to be succeeded by a 'team leader' or co-ordinator concept. Significantly the empirical data of my study gave over-whelming evidence that the present role culture of Hodson High School created 'barriers' by departmental insularity, thus prohibiting cross-curricular and all-school developments, as well as inhibiting management practices. However, even if a 'team leader' concept succeeded an apparently out-dated head of department role, management skills would still be required by those teachers taking on management roles and their training needs met. Perhaps in future due recognition will be given to the middle management role of heads of department in status, time allocation and training.

No longer can the role be perceived in the narrow perspective of a subject head, which was the case in 1956. The middle manager in schools, like his counterpart in industry, must be able to manage change and if needs be lead effectively a task force set up on a temporary basis to solve specific problems. The evolving role and limited research on the role of heads of department have blurred the training needs of heads of department and it must not be assumed that trainers have the intuition to provide the appropriate training they perceive heads of department require to be effective in their work.


## Appointment of Middle Managers

The apparently established custom and practice of appointing heads of department was to assume that effective master teachers would make good middle managers. This was a peculiar way of creating strong middle management in schools; indeed,

## Conclusions

the assumption that a head of department should be both master teacher and middle manager is a questionable nonsense. Classroom teachers may not have the potential to be effective heads of department, and therefore should remain with a full commitment to the prime activity of the school: helping students to learn.

When master teachers were appointed as middle managers at Hodson High School it seemed strange that they were not initiated into the management skills they required, rather than be allowed to flounder, creating for themselves much stress and anxiety. This suggestion of training assumes that their needs are identified, either by the role occupant, his super-ordinates, or may be by his peer group and appropriate facilities be provided to meet these needs. My research findings are a firm basis upon which training needs may be met, for it must not be assumed that potential heads of department have acquired management skills to lead their departments.


## Professional Autonomy and Training

A tradition prevailed amongst teachers of working in isolation in their classrooms, and they were wary of allowing performance appraisal to occur. An assumption was made by the majority of heads of department that following a teachers' initial training course it was a matter of practice which perfected the art of teaching. Unfortunately, an autonomous stance frequently formed a barrier between teachers, concealing weaknesses and fears, and prohibited a programme of professional development occurring supported by appropriate training. It was also noted that heads of department did not perceive themselves as staff developers, appraisers or evaluators, all three roles being a possible means of identifying the training needs of individuals and/or of themselves.

Professional autonomy manifestly stifled the potential for training to become a recognized professional activity for all

## Conclusions

teachers. It was not surprising therefore that there was no well integrated programme of continuing training for teachers at Hodson High School or in any of the pilot study schools.

> The concept that managerial skills become progressively more important with seniority, and are required to a limited extent by even the most callow student teacher, should be introduced into the professional ethos of teachers (Duffett, 1982).

To ensure that such a provision is made, training must become an integral and recognized part of the concept of pro-fessionalism. Such an expectation will not be realized over-night, but a key to its realization could be effectively trained middle managers, as senior management alone would be unable to cope with the demands for such a task within schools. However, teachers need to have a clear understanding of their role and an appreciation that training is an integral part of professional development, but, as a head of department perceived:

> ...providing INSET doesn't necessarily make any difference ... it all depends upon the frame of mind of participants. You can help people, but can only take them so far. It is a truism that a school is a place where some students and teachers learn and some don't ... this goes for heads of department

## Management Training for Heads of Department

Having highlighted the perceptions of heads of departments' major training needs, it is important to re- iterate that Hodson High School was considered by many professionals and parents to be a very good school with a strong commitment from the staff to maintain high standards of professionalism. It was through the process of penetrating the veneer of the 'taken-for-granted' aspects of the role of departmental head and the school's organization that the data for these

# Conclusions

findings came to light. Beneath the veneer of 'all is well' was displayed the fears of post-holders who were keen to be successful middle managers but had not received training to rectify their perceived weaknesses. The lack of practice of negotiation was found to be the major contributor to the ineffective management practices of heads of department. The implications of delegation, appraisal and evaluation, change and innovation, team building and time management, were the other major perceived needs of the heads of department, as they emerged from the ethnographic process of the study, which in turn have implications for the school, the L.E.A. and the Government.

## Implications for Heads of Department

### i) Accepting a Middle Management Role

Heads of department needed to perceive their present and/or future roles in management terms. There was a general lack of understanding amongst heads of department about the significance of management and a reluctance to accept their role as middle managers, preferring instead to be master teachers.

### ii) Perceiving and Fulfilling Training Needs

Effective training in the first instance depends on individuals perceiving a need for training. Many of the heads of department in the study fell into Hoyle's heuristic category of 'Restricted Professional' where they chose to opt out of professional training because they were afraid to admit to incompetence. This stance did not contribute towards the establishment of heads of department as middle managers.

Furthermore, training as a concept and practice had not been accepted by most heads of department as an integral part of a professional career development. However, they believed that regular staff appraisal could be the means of identifying training needs.

167

# Conclusions

### iii) Planning Training Based on Identified Needs

An undue emphasis given to an intuitive approach to management and a belief which was held by the majority of heads of department at Hodson High School that management skills will develop through experience in post was demonstrated to be false.

### iv) Need for a Negotiator Role

Possibly the most important role for heads of department was that of a negotiator, for this role underpinned most of the major management practices thay required to become effective in their work. Indeed, the role of negotiator could cause heads of department to comprehend the paradigm within which they may perceive their role, for the great majority of heads of department at Hodson High School had not seriously considered the various paradigms of organizations and their role within the school organization.

### v) Finding Job Satisfaction

A lack of management training contributed towards minimizing job satisfaction for heads of department and created a feeling of being 'burnt out'. A lack of confidence in wishing to be a middle manager and having preference for fulfilling the role of a master teacher, for which they believed that they had been trained, also contributed towards much frustration and stress and a feeling of being squeezed between departmental members and senior management.

### vi) Providing Staff Development and Education of Quality

Heads of department considered that they had a responsibility to their departmental colleagues and for the quality of education provided for students. This responsibility required them to be effective appraisers, delegators, evaluators, negotiators, team builders and managers of change and time in

# Conclusions

which the great majority demonstrated poor practice.

vii) Fulfilling Training Needs

In order to fulfil training needs of heads of department it is assumed that schools and L.E.As. have the means of providing effective training facilities.

# Implications for Schools

i) Providing an Induction Course

In the study, heads of department desired an induction course for their peers as a recognition that their role was sufficiently important to warrant training. When heads of department took up new posts it was assumed by senior management and departmental members that they had already acquired skills to lead a team of professional teachers in the pursuit of educating students. These assumptions were false. A planned induction course would create not only a forum in which a concept of training might be established in schools, but could be the means of meeting identified needs of individuals, starting with those needs noted at appointment interviews.

ii) Creating a Job Description

A job description which ensures that teachers receive a clear communication of their responsibilities and S.M.T. expectations is essential for effective management. The process of interpreting role definitions can be a means of S.M.T. identifying training needs of role occupants, a basis for staff appraisal, and for heads of department an instrument for evaluating their work. Empirical data showed that heads of department welcomed a clear job description to promote their awareness of S.M.T. expectations of them.

iii) Accepting the Notion of Professional Development

## Conclusions

A commitment to the notion of professional development throughout a teacher's career requires a school professional development policy and a planned programme or approach to training for all members of staff. (see D.E.S., 1985a). Such an approach was desired by many departmental members and most heads of department in the study but the framework in which such an approach might become a reality was not apparent. Although the provision of training is no guarantee for the effective performance of an individual's role, training for a management role gives the opportunity to improve their performance and to increase job satisfaction.

iv) Devising a Training Programme

To provide 'on the job training' complemented by 'off the job' skills-based activities could be an effective contribution to the development of middle managers. However, the assumption that heads of department are able to transfer skills to a school environment may not be made, for they will need guidance in such practices.

School based training was advocated in the James Report (1972) and by others since, for example, Ballinger (1984) who argued that the most effective influence on job performance was specific training based on the job itself. This thesis assumed that training needs were identified, and that provision of training and an evaluation of work was a reality. Equally an active research tradition based on an individual's capability to reflect upon their actions and to act upon their reflections assumes that a school ethos and organization is created to cause such activities to occur.

v) Challenging Teacher Professional Autonomy

INSET recruits chosen from those who volunteer for specific training avoids confronting those who choose to refrain from training courses. Nomination of individuals based on specific needs would limit the professional autonomy of teachers, but couls be advantageous in meeting both school and individual

## Conclusions

needs. This latter scenario assumes that a school's management team has the means to identify teacher training needs. A school's teacher appraisal scheme, as an integral part of a staff development approach could be the means of identifying training needs as could the process of effective team building by heads of department. An on-going process of staff appraisal could certainly create positive attitudes towards professional training and start to meet the demands of training needs of teachers which have accrued over the past years.

vi) Having sufficient resources

Schools need the facility to plan the release of teachers from timetabled commitments. Based on the findings of this study many heads of department required extended courses of training. However, short bursts of intensive work, such as those observed on TRIST activities or even half day sessions spent on such down-to-earth topics as target-setting, the art of chairing meetings or keeping departmental records could be of much benefit. The fact remains, schools have to plan and co-ordinate the release of teachers for such courses, and not prejudice the quality of education offered to students in that process. The flexibility within the organization of Hodson High School to achieve such objectives was not possible, particularly in respect of the heavy teaching loads carried by heads of department owing to the staffing levels of the school.

## Implications for the L.E.A.

i) Making adequate provision for teacher training

Both the D.E.S. publications, "Teaching Quality" (1983a) and "Better Schools" (1985a) point out that managing the teaching force, fostering professionalism and the provision for a wide spectrum of training is the responsibility of the L.E.A. There was much evidence in the study that in-service training

171

# Conclusions

held little appeal because many teachers were reluctant to give up their own time: they received little or no financial support for training, and it was considered unreasonable to expect them to attend courses after school hours. This raised the question of L.E.A.s granting sufficient time and finances for teachers to be involved in training, acknowledging that they have financial constraints within which they have to work.

Time and again a comparison was made by interviewees in the study between the provision of training in schools and industry, where in the latter situation it was believed appropriate time and finances were provided. Post April 1987 L.E.A.s make bids to the D.E.S. for INSET funding; those bids must be realistic and not based on past tradition and practice.

## ii) Providing experimental management practice

As potential course providers it is important that courses undertaken should be experiential so that management theory has a better chance of being related to practice. A consideration of management practice could well lead to an awareness of theory, and an analysis of such training needs identified. It may not be assumed that a curriculum development course focussing upon the skills, concepts and knowledge of a specific subject area of the curriculum will not require the highlighting of management skills in order to implement curriculum development effectively.

## iii) Choosing a model for INSET

Most L.E.A.s appear to support an INSET model favouring a high degree of teacher autonomy, where individuals direct their own professional development. For effective management training to occur for all teachers, L.E.A.s need to initiate changes which have political consequences for all parties involved in INSET.

# Conclusions

a) Training relevant to job performance:
b) Preparation before, and support after training:
c) A reduction in the autonomy of course providers.

iv) Making realistic assumptions about INSET

Networks set up within L.E.A.s whereby colleagues from different schools may aid the transfer of good management practices and a data bank of perceived examples of good practice can assist both schools and individuals in meeting training needs. A D.E.S. (1984b) document reporting on the work of an L.E.A. suggested that the inadequacy of the advisory service had resulted in failing to sustain the L.E.A.s curriculum development initiatives. It was further noted that the INSET available was unrelated to the needs of the schools.

The L.E.A.'s role within the government's new L.E.A. Training Grants Scheme (1987) of provider and enabler of INSET, assume that training needs are identified and/or predicted with curriculum and examination reforms. This was a fallacy noted at Hodson High School, particularly as it affected departmental head's management performance.

## Implications for the Government

i) Providing sufficient resources for training middle managers

It has been acknowledged that:

It is the head of department next to headteachers who have as a group potentially the greatest influence on the quality of work within a comprehensive school (Welsh Office, 1984)

A N.F.E.R. project also draws attention to:

## Conclusions

The important role middle management can play in
encouraging or obstructing curricular and other
desired changes (Educ. Research News No.44, 1986).

Suffice it to say there has been a gross mismatch between the
D.E.S. expectations of heads of department and its financial
support to fund management courses to meet their perceived
needs.

ii) Recognizing the importance of a middle management role in
schools

The Government has yet to recognize fully the importance of
the role of middle managers in secondary schools by actually
providing adequate time in which they may manage their
departments. H.M.I. have acknowledged many times that an
increasing amount of staff time for management tasks must be
provided during the school day: for example, see D.E.S.,
1979, and D.E.S., 1985a, but this acknowledgement has not
been matched by realistic financial resources. A target
comparable with the Canadian scene, to provide fifty per cent
of a timetabled week for heads of department to perform their
management tasks would be a realistic proposition.

iii) Integrating training with professional development

The Teachers' Pay and Conditions Act 1987 provides the
opportunity for INSET during all or part of five days each
year when teachers are not required to teach students.
However, after a long tradition of assumptions about the role
and capability of heads of department to lead effectively a
department, the status of training for heads of department
within a profession must be raised by providing time and
facilities comparable to that afforded middle managers in
industry. This would have both a marked effect on the
performance of heads of department in the teaching profession
and the quality of education provided for students.

I hope that the contents of this book have caused both senior

174

## Conclusions

managers, middle managers and aspiring heads of department to look beneath the surface of the taken-for-granted reality of the every day life of their schools. This will include the assumptions, fears, problems and aspirations of colleagues in a profession where there is more or less mobility of staff from one school to another. At this time of continual curriculum change much dependence is thrust upon the managerial and professional skills of heads of department. I trust that the findings of my study will give clear indications of the provision actually required to meet the training needs of middle managers in secondary school. Appropriate management training in schools is yet to come of age.

# BIBLIOGRAPHY

Abrahamson, M. (1967) <u>The Professional in the Organisation</u>. Chicago: Rand McNally.

Adair, J. (1979) <u>Training for Leadership</u>. Aldershot: Gower Press.

Adams, N. (1986) <u>Secondary School Management Today</u>. London: Hutchinson.

Alexander, Sir W. (1945 - 1967) <u>The Burnham Primary and Secondary Reports</u> - London: London Councils and Education Press.

Alexander, W. (1954) <u>Education in England</u>. London: Newnes Educational Publications.

Archer, J.F. (1981) The Role of the Head of Department with Specific Reference to the Staff Development Aspect. M.A. Thesis. New University of Ulster. Unpublished.

Argyris, C. (1964) <u>Integrating and the Organisation</u>. New York: John Wiley.


Bailey, P.J.M. (1973) The functons of heads of department in Comprehensive Schools. <u>Journal of Educational Administration and history</u>, 4 (1).

Ballinger, E. (1982) The Politics of Establishing an Innovatory Management Role. <u>Educational Management & Administration</u>, 10 (2).

Ballinger, E. (1984) <u>Management Development Outside</u> Education: <u>Some Implications for the N.D.C.</u> Bristol: National Development Centre.

Barnes, B.B. (1974) <u>Scientific Knowledge and Sociological Theory</u>. London: Routledge and Kegan Paul.

Baron, G. (1975) Approaches to Educational Administration as a Field of Study, Research and Application. In Hughes, M.(ed) <u>Administering Education: International Challenge</u>. London: Athlone Press.

Bates, A.W. (1970) The Administration of Comprehensive Schools with particular reference to the relationship between the work of teachers and the kind of Comprehensive School in which they serve. Ph.D. University of Leicester. Unpublished.

Bayne-Jardine, C. C. & Hanham, C. (1972) Heads of
Department. Forum, 15, (1), p 26.

Bayne-Jardine, C. C. (1986) Staff Development. In
Marland, M. (ed) School Management Skills. London:
Heinemann.

Becher, T. & Maclure, S. (1978) Accountability in
Education. Slough: NFER.

Becher, T. (1981) Politics for Educational
Accountability. London: Heinemann.

Bennis, W.G. 1969. Organisational Development- Its
Nature Origins and Prospects. New York: Addison
Wesley.

Bennis, W., Benne, K., & Chin, R.(eds) (1971) The
Management of Change. London: Holt Rinehart & Winston.

Best, R. (1983) Education and Care. London: Heinemann.

Beveridge, W.E. (1975) The Interview in Staff
Appraisal. London: Allen and Unwin.

Blackburn, K. (1986) Teacher Appraisal. In Marland, M.
(ed) School Management Skills. London: Heinemann.

Bloomer R.G. (1980) The Role of the Head of Department
- Some Questions and Answers. Educational Research, 22
(2) pp 83-96.

Bloomer, R.G. (1980) The Role of the Head of Department
- Some Questions and Answers. Educational Research, 22
2) pp 83-96).

Bolam, R. (1975) The Management of Educational Change:
Towards a Conceptual framework. In Houghton. V. (ed)
Managemnt in Education. London: Ward Lock.

Brown, I.G.E. (1984) Split-site secondary schools and
the role of the head of department: some problems and
possibilities. Aspects of Education, 33. pp 34-35.

Brydson, P. (1983) Head of Department and Self
Evaluation. Hull: Institute of Education.

Burns, T. and Stalker, G.M. (1968) The Management of
Innovation. London: Tavistock Publications.

Burrell, G. and Morgan, G. (1979) Sociological
Paradigms and Organisational Analysis. London:
Heinemann.

Bush, T. (1980) Approaches to School Management.
London: Harper and Row.

Campbell, R.J. 1984. In-School Development: The Role of the
Curriculum Postholder. School Organisation. 4 (4).

Chamberlain, R.N. (1982) An investigation into the
development and functions of the posts of heads of
departments in Comprehensive Schools. M.A. University of
Hull. Unpublished.

Chamberlain, R.N. (1984) The Comprehensive head of
department. Aspects of Education, 33. pp 18-25.

Chilton, J.C. (1985) The Staff meeting in the Structure of
Secondary School Management. M.A. Manchester University.
Unpublished.

Chin, R. & Benne, K.D. (1969) General strategies for
effecting change in human systems. In Bennis, W.G. (ed) The
Planning of Change. London: Holt, Rinehart & Winston.

Cockcroft, W.H. (1982) Mathematics Counts. Report of the
Committee of Enquiry into the Teaching of Mathematics in
Schools. London: HMSO.

Cohen, L. (1970) School, Size and Heads Bureaucratic Role
Conception. Educational Research. 23.

Cox, C.B. & Bryson, R. (eds) 1977. Black Papers 1977.
London: Temple Smith.


Davies, B. (1983) Head of Department involvement in
decisions. Educational Management and Administration. 11.

Day, C. (1984) The role of a head of department in staff
development. British Journal of In-Service Education. 1(2).

Day, C. & Moore, R. (eds) Staff Development in the Secondary
School. London: Croom Helm.

Dennison, W.F. (1981) Education in Jeopardy. Oxford:
Blackwell.

Dennison, W.F. (1985) Flexible Structures and Secondary
Schools. Educational Management and Administration. 13.

D.E.S. (1977a) Ten Good Schools: A Secondary School Enquiry.
        London: HMSO
    - (1977b) Curriculum 11-13. London: HMSO.
    - (1978) Making INSET Work. London.: HMSO.
    - (1979) Aspects of Secondary Education in
        England. London: HMSO.

D.E.S. (1981a) The School Curriculum. London: HMSO.
  - (1981b) Curriculum 11-16: A Review of Progress.
    London: HMSO.
  - (1981c) Circular 6/81 The School Curriculum. London:
    HMSO.
  - (1982) The New Teacher in School. London: HMSO.
  - (1983a) Teaching Quality. Cmnd 8836.
    London: HMSO.
  - (1983b) Circular 3/83 The In-Service Teacher
    Training Grants Scheme. London: HMSO.
  - (1984a) Education Observed. A review of the first six
    months of published reports by H.M.
    Inspectors. London: HMSO.
  - (1984b) Report on H.M. Inspectors on Educational
    Provision and Response in some Norfolk
    Schools. London: HMSO.
  - (1985a) Better Schools. Cmnd 9469. London: HMSO.
  - (1985b) Quality in Schools: Evaluation and
    Appraisal. London: HMSO.
  - (1986) The 1986 Education Act. London: HMSO.
Deitscher, I. (1973) What we say; What we do. Illinois:
  Scott Foreman.
Drucker, P.F. (1980) Managing in Turbulent Times. London:
  Pan Books.
Duffett, R.H.H. (1982) Study of Devolution of Managerial
  Responsibility to Heads of Schools. Cambridge:
  Cambridgeshire County Council.
Dunham, J. (1978) Change and Stress in the Head of
  Department's Role. Educational Research, 21 (1) pp 44-47.
Dyer, W.F. (1977) Teambuilding Issues and Alternatives. New
  York: Addison Wesley.

Earley, P. & Fletcher-Campbell, F. (1986) Developed
  Professional or Professional Developer? The Changing
  Requirements of Departmental Heads. Slough: NFER.
Elms, D. (1982) The role of the head of department in INSET.
  In Bolam, R. (ed) School Focussed In-Service Training.
  London: Heinemann.
Encyclopaedia of Educational Research. (1982) Fifth Edition.
  London: Macmillan.

179

Ends, E.J. and Page, C.W. (1977) Organisational Team Building.
Cambridge Mass.: Winthrop Press.

England, E.E. (1980) The Role of the Head of Department. M.A.
Thesis. New University of Ulster. Unpublished.

Etzioni, A. (1964) Modern Organisations. Englewood Cliffs, N.J.:
Prentice-Hall.

Everard, K.B. 1984. Management in Comprehensive Schools. What can
be learned from industry? York: Centre for the Study of
Comprehensive Schools, University of York.

Everard, K.B. (1986) Developing Management in School. Oxford:
Blackwell.

Everard, K.B. & Morris, G. (1985) Effective School Management.
London: Harper & Row.


Fletcher-Campbell, F. (1986) Middle Management in Schools. Heads
of Department: An Annotated Bibliography. Slough: NFER.

Fullan, M. (1982) The Meaning of Educational Change. Ontario:
OISE.


Glaser, B.G. and Strauss, A.L. (1967) The Disovery of Grounded
Theory. London: Weidenfeld and Nicolson.

Glatter, R. (1972) Management Development for the Education
Profession. London: Harrap.

Glatter, R. (1973) Off-The-Job Staff Development in Education. In
Pratt, S. (ed) Staff Development in Education. London: Councils
& Education Press.

Glatter, R. (1976) Staff Development in and out of School.
Secondard Education. 6 (2).

Glatter, R. (1982) The Micropolitics of Education: Issues for
training. Educational Management and Administration. 10 (2)

Goffman, E. (1968) Asylums. Harmondsworth: Penguin.

Goffman, E. (1969) Where the Action is. Harmondsworth: Penguin
Press.

Goffman, E. (1972) Relations in Public. Harmondsworth: Penguin.

Goffman, E. (1975) The Presentation of Self for Everyday Life.
Harmondsworth: Penguin.

Gordon, P. (1985) Is Teaching a Profession. Bedford Way Papers
25.

Gosden, P.H. (1972) The Evolution of a Profession. Oxford:
Blackwell.

Gosden, P.H. 1983. The Education System Since 1944. London: Robertson.

Gray, H.L. (1982) School as an Organisation. Driffield: Nafferton.

Greenfield, T.B. (1975) Theory about Organisation: A New Perspecive and the Implications for School. In Houghton.V.(ed) Management in Education. London: Ward Lock/ Open University Press.

Greenfield, T.B. (1980) Theory about Organisation. In Bush, T. Approaches to Secondary School Management. London: Harper & Row.

Gross, N. (1966) Exploration in Role Analysis. London: John Wiley.

Gross, N. Implementing Organisational Innovations. London and New York: Harper and Row.

Hall, J.C. & Thomas, J.B. (1977) Mathematics Departmental Headship in Secondary Schools. Educational Administration,5 (2).

Handy, C. (1987) Gods of Management. London: Pan Books.

Handy, C. (1981) Understanding Organisations. Harmondsworth: Penguin.

Handy, C. (1984) Taken for Granted? Understanding Schools as Organisations. London: Longmans/Schools Council.

Hodgkinson, C. (1983) The Philosophy of Leadership. Oxford: Blackwell.

Houghton, V. (ed) (1976) Management in Education. London: Ward Lock.

Howson, J. (1980) Perceptions on the post of Head of Department in Comprehensive Schools. M.Sc Thesis. University of Oxford. Unpublished.

Hoyle, E. (1969) Organisation Theory and Educational Administration. In Baron G. & Taylor, W. (eds) Educational Administration and the Social Sciences. London: Athlone Press.

Hoyle, E. (1970) Planned Organisational Change in Education. Research in Education, 3.

Hoyle, E. (1974) Professionality, Professionalism and Control in Teaching. Educational Review, 3 (2).

Hoyle, E. (1986) The Politics of School Management. London: Hodder and Stoughton.

Hughes, M.G. (ed) Administering Education: The International Challenge. London: Athlone Press.

Hughes, M.G.(Ed) Managing Education. London and New York:
Holt, Rinehart and Winston.

ILEA (1984) Improving Secondary Schools. Report of a
Committee of Enquiry chaired By Hargreaves, D.H.. London:
Inner London Education Authority.

Katz, D. and Kahn, R.L. (1966) The Social Psychology of
Organisations. New York: Wiley.

Lacey, C. (1970) Problems of Sociological Fieldwork. In
Shipman, M. The Organisation and Impact of Social Research.
London: Routledge and Kegan Paul.
Lambert, K. (1972) The Role of the Head of Department in
Schools. MA Thesis. University of Southampton. Unpublished.
Lindsey County Council. (1970) A Survey of Head of
Department posts in seventy L.E.A.'s. Lindsey County
Council.
Lofland, J. (1971) Analysing Social Settings. A Guide to
Qualitative Observation and Analysis. Belmont, California:
Wadsworth.

Macpherson, R.J.S. (1984) On being and Becoming an
Educational Administrator: some Methodological Issues.
Educational Administration Quarterly. Fall 1984.
Marland, M. (1971) Head of Department. London: Heinneman.
Marland, M and Hill, S. (Eds) (1981) Departmental
Management. London: Heineman.
McGivering, I.C. (1971) Organisation. In Kemper, T. (ed) A
Handbook of Management. Harmondsworth: Penguin.
McGregor, D. (1960) The Human Side of Enterprise. New York:
McGraw-Hill.
Midgley, J.B. (1980) Middle Management in Secondary Schools.
M.Ed. Thesis. University of Bristol. Unpublished.

Nuttall, D. (1981) School Self Evaluation. London: Schools
Council.

Paisley, A.H. and Paisley, T.J. (1980) The Question of Style in Educational Management. Educational Administration.9 (1)

Paisley, A.H. (1981) Organisation and Management. York: Longman.

Parlett, M. and Hamilton, D. (1972) Evaluation as Illumination: A New Approach to the Study of Innovative Programmes. Occasional Paper No.9. University of Edinburgh: Centre for Research in the Educational Sciences.

Randle, R.R. (1984) Teachers in Dual Roles. Aspects of Education, 33 pp 46-56.

Ribbins, P. (1985) The Role of the Middle Manager in the Secondary School. In Hughes, M. Managing Education: The System and the Institution. London and New York: Holt, Rinehard and Winston.

Richardson, E. (1973) The Teacher, the School and the Task of Management. London: Heinneman.

Rodger, I.A. (1983) Teachers with Posts of Responsibility in Primary Schools. Durham: University School of Education.

Scriven, M. (1967) The Methodology of Evaluation. In Tyler, R.W. Perspectives of Curriculum Evaluation. Chicago: Rand McNally.

Siddle, J. (1977) The Concept of the Head of Department as a Middle Manager with Specific Reference to Comprehensive School Science Departments. M.Ed THesis. Leicester University. Unpublished.

Silverman, D. (1970) The Theory of Organisations. London: Heinneman.

Smith, I. (1977) Ten Secondary Schools: A Study of School and Departmental Management. MA Thesis. University of Dundee. Unpublished.

Stake, R. (1980) The Case Study Method in Social Enquiry. In Simons, H. (ed) Towards a Science of the Singular. Norwich: University of East Anglia.

Steinmetz, L.L. (1985) Managing the Marginal & Unsatifactory Performer. Read ing Mass: Addison Wesley.

Straker, N. (1984) The Teaching Load of a Head of
Mathematics and Consequent Effects on the Department.
School Organisation, 4. 3 pp 221-29.

Suffolk Education Department. (1985) Those Having Torches:
Teacher Appraisal. Suffolk County Council.

Suffolk Education Department. (1987) In the Light of
Torches: Teacher Appraisal. Suffolk County Council.

Tawney, D. (ed) (1976) Curriculum Evaluation Today: Trends
and Implications. London: Macmillan.

Taylor, W. (1964) Role Functions of College Principals.
Sociological Review, 12 (2).

Tropp, A. (1957) The School Teachers. London: Heinneman.

Waters, S. (1985) The Role of the Director of English. Paper
presented at BEMAS Seminar on Research in the Management
and Administration of Secondary Education. Sheffield: City
Polytechnic.

Welsh Office. (1984) Departmental Organisation in Secondary
Schools. H.M.I. Occasional Paper. Welsh Office.

Wheeler, G. (1973). In Taylor, P.H. and Walton, J. (eds) The
Curriculum, Research, Innovation and Change. London: Ward
Lock.

Woods, P. (1983) Sociology and the School. London: Routledge
and Kegan Paul.

Woods, P. (1986) Inside Schools: Ethnography in Educational
Research. London: Routledge and Kegan Paul.